"This is a unique book that is … d with the fate of Chinese worke… - filtered voices about their expe… China, recorded from multiple … or not to strike, their initial enthusiasm, their distrust of their peers and representatives, internal divisions, and the uncertainty of what to do next. No academic treatise could possibly capture the circumstances and state of mind of Chinese workers as well as this book."

—Anita Chan, coeditor of *The China Journal*

"The global economic crisis has intensified class struggle all around the world. In China, the party-state has strengthened repression over workers who go on strike and their supporters in an effort to maintain industrial peace and facilitate industrial relocation as economic growth has slowed. Through detailed case studies and in-depth interviews with workers, this timely book shows how Chinese migrant workers defend their labor rights and struggle to survive through large-scale political and economic restructuring."

—Chris King-Chi Chan, City University of Hong Kong

"*Striking to Survive* brilliantly documents the struggles in the past few years of China's migrant workers in two major factories in the Pearl River Delta at the center of the world's workshop. The testimonies of their precious experiences challenge the prevalent nationalist narrative about 'Chinese workers stealing American jobs' and illustrate that Chinese workers are fighting similar battles against neoliberalism as workers everywhere else."

—Hsiao-Hung Pai, author of
Scattered Sand: The Story of China's Rural Migrants

"Leftists of all persuasions must try to come to grips with questions about the Chinese labor movement. Is China a capitalist economy? A state-capitalist economy? Will the emerging Chinese labor movement necessarily take the form of decentralized, local upheavals? If so, will that doom the movement to defeat or might it assist Chinese workers in avoiding the bureaucratic business unionism common in the West? Haymarket Books is to be congratulated for making it possible for rank-and-file Chinese workers to tell us their stories."

—Staughton Lynd, coeditor with Alice Lynd of *Rank and File: Personal Histories by Working-Class Organizers*

"*Striking to Survive* uses testimonies of leaders in two strikes in China to give us a window into why and how workers, with little training or support, boldly took collective action against their employers. Unlike most existing literature that observes Chinese labor relations from a distance, these oral histories take us deep into the nitty-gritty of each step in the disputes, as the participants lay bare the quandaries and frustrations they experienced at each turn. Experienced labor organizers will recognize that there is incredible potential in the collective agency of the workers, which is ultimately threatened by the lack of effective labor market institutions that satisfactorily address workers' concerns. This book is an important read for anyone who seriously wants to understand workers in China today."

—**Katie Quan, Senior Fellow, UC Berkeley Center for Labor Research and Education**

"As American workers get stripped of union contracts and bargaining rights, more will be forced to rely on strike activity—in the absence of any supportive legal framework. Labor militants abroad, like the author of *Striking to Survive*, know a lot about this difficult terrain, since they daily risk police harassment and imprisonment for organizing work stoppages. This book is a 'Chinese import' with much to teach US rank and filers. Its invaluable lessons—on strike tactics, strategy, and workplace committee building—are a 'just-in-time' delivery."

—**Steve Early, former CWA strike organizer and author of *Save Our Unions: Dispatches From A Movement in Distress***

Striking to Survive

Workers' Resistance to Factory Relocations in China

By Fan Shigang
Translated by Henry Moss

Haymarket Books
Chicago, Illinois

Published in 2018 by
Haymarket Books
P.O. Box 180165
Chicago, IL 60618
773-583-7884
www.haymarketbooks.org
info@haymarketbooks.org

ISBN: 978-1-60846-909-3

Trade distribution:
In the US, Consortium Book Sales and Distribution,
www.cbsd.com
In Canada, Publishers Group Canada, www.pgcbooks.ca
In the UK, Turnaround Publisher Services,
www.turnaround-uk.com
All other countries, Ingram Publisher Services International,
IPS_Intlsales@ingramcontent.com

This book was published with the generous support of Lannan
Foundation and Wallace Action Fund.

Cover design by Rachel Cohen. Cover image © Stringer, AP
Images, of workers from Sui Bao Security Transport Co. on
strike for higher salaries, blocking a road in Guangzhou, south
China's Guangdong province in February 2014.

Printed in Canada by union labor.

Library of Congress Cataloging-in-Publication
data is available.

10 9 8 7 6 5 4 3 2 1

Table of Contents

The Third Round of Migrant Labor Struggles in Post-Socialist Guangdong:

Introduction to the English edition

Pun Ngai and Sam Austin

The global resurgence of right-wing populism associated with figures such as Trump in the United States, Putin in Russia, and Modi in India reflects, among other things, the combination of mass resentment against "globalism" (what the left used to call "neoliberal globalization") and frustration with repeated betrayals by nominally left-leaning politicians. In the United States, in particular, one sentiment that unites the new populist right with many supporters of the new populist left (associated with Bernie Sanders and the Democratic Socialists of America) is the desire to "save our jobs"—from "Communist" China, among other imagined threats.

But is "China" stealing jobs from the United States—or any other country, for that matter? Many other commentators have pointed out that relatively few manufacturing jobs have moved from the United States to China.[1] The high tide of out-sourcing took place in the 1980s, when many manufacturing jobs moved from cities in the northern United States to places such as Mexico, Taiwan, and other parts of the United States with weaker unions and lower wages. Many other jobs were replaced by automation. If mainland China "stole" jobs from anyone, it was not from the United States but from Mexico and parts of East Asia in the 1990s and 2000s. But now, in 2017, protectionists in even those countries have lost much of the material basis for China-bashing. Just as automobile workers in Detroit are held responsible for "pushing capital out of town" by demanding a dignified way of life, the new generation of workers in China's "workshop of the world"—the Pearl River Delta (PRD)—have significantly pushed wages up over the last fifteen years. This, combined with real estate speculation, with-drawal of government tax benefits and infrastructure subsidies, higher social welfare packets, and fierce interfirm competition, has driven firms to poorer parts of China or other countries such as Bangladesh, Cambodia, and Myanmar.

This book documents the struggles of Chinese workers against such "outsourcing" in two factories: one supplying furniture for transnational corporations such as Walmart and the other supplying garments for the Japanese clothing brand Uniqlo. Both illustrate that Chinese workers are not only *not* stealing American (or Mexican or Korean) jobs, but are ac-tually engaged in similar struggles against capital's incessant flight to ever-cheaper locations (which often means places with even more oppressive regimes and exploitative conditions). One reason this book has been translated into English is to challenge the anti-Chinese and essentially nationalist narrative of protectionism common among both right and left wings of the political spectrum in the United States and beyond, and in its place to foster an awareness of what workers of all countries share in common—including experiences of resistance that might provide lessons for workers elsewhere.

This is the second book presenting English translations of workers' accounts collected by the activists behind the underground Chinese periodical, *Factory Stories* (*Gongchang Longmenzhen*).[2] The first book, also published by Haymarket Press last year as *China on Strike: Narratives of Workers' Resistance*, presented firsthand accounts of fifteen different struggles in the PRD from what the group calls the first and second rounds or waves (*chao*) of postsocialist migrant labor struggles in the region, spanning the first decade of the twenty-first century. This second book, on the other hand, consists mainly of nine workers' accounts of a single strike from the third round of struggles, dating from late 2012 through 2016. In addition to these accounts and the main author's analytical introduction, this English edition also includes a detailed overview of another comparable struggle from this period, plus a new preface in which one of the authors contextualizes the book for Anglophone readers.

Both of the struggles described in this book were typical of this "third round" of labor unrest. The participants were older, most having settled down with their families in apartments they rented near the factories—in contrast with many of the protagonists of *China on Strike*, who were young, single workers living in factory dormitories, and who planned to move back to their rural hometowns after a few years. Consistent with this change in demographics and living conditions, both of the struggles recounted here were centered on different goals, reflecting the workers' different attitudes toward their jobs. Whereas the first round was largely centered on wage arrears, and the second expanded to add demands such as wage raises and even union reform, this third round centered on demands for severance pay and Social Insurance. This change of demands reflects not only the older age of participants, but also what might be the most important characteristic of this third round of struggles: the fact that most were sparked by the relocation of factories from central PRD cities such as Shenzhen to cheaper cities nearby (such as Huizhou), cheaper provinces in central and western China, or cheaper countries elsewhere in Asia. This last factor seems to mark a decisive break with the previous two rounds of struggles, since the workers had little hope of improving their situation within their workplaces, but instead aimed only at a last-ditch effort of getting all they could before they had to retire or look for other jobs, probably outside the manufacturing sector, which is shrinking in these cities, or upgrading in ways that exclude workers without a higher level of education and training.

Labor Militancy in China

Thanks to the records of strikes provided by militant workers and their supporters, we are able to make sense of the changing collective actions of China's new working class. As a result of thirty years of reform, the repositioning of China as a "workshop of the world" in the age of globalization provided the bedrock for nurturing a new Chinese working class. In spite of the dominance of a "post-class" ideology of dog-eat-dog competition among individuals, collective power of the business community, institutional barriers from the state, and lack of support from other sectors of society, this new laboring class is fighting to defend itself through a variety of struggles in its workplaces.

Despite the neoliberal project in China and worldwide to submerge the existence of class, the new generation of the working class carries out various forms of collective action. The Chinese state has never publicly released comprehensive strike data, but sources such as *China Labour Bulletin* have compiled and analyzed data that support anecdotal accounts of growing collective actions among migrant workers pursuing delayed wages, demanding compensation for factory relocation, or pressuring enterprises to increase wages and living allowances.[3]

These actions include litigation, such as suing subcontractors, as well as collective actions such as sit-ins, strikes, and even threatening or committing suicide. Workers have confronted capital at the point of production in the workplace as well as challenging power at societal levels in the courtroom, on the street, or in front of government buildings.

It is now estimated that more than 280 million migrant workers from the countryside are working in China's urban and peri-urban industrial areas, with the number increasing every year. With the inflow of transnational capital and the restructuring of domestic capital, postsocialist China has become characterized by the severe exacerbation of class stratification and interclass conflicts. As part of China's economic reforms starting in 1978, Deng Xiaoping and his followers strove to legitimize governance by replacing class struggle with law and related institutions as an arena to mediate conflict through the courts rather than in the streets. New legal provisions passed since 2008, tested by workers in the labor dispute arbitration committees and courts, were said to contribute to raising worker consciousness of labor rights. Yet, while workers continue to proclaim adherence to the law, they have by no means constrained their activities to the legal terrain: when the system fails them, workers still take to the streets.

Some collective actions are accompanied by sentiments against foreign capital and a discourse of workers' rights, which are then interpreted as "political" as well as economic. However, the cases documented here primarily concern *Chinese* capital (albeit to supply goods for American and Japanese corporations), so they illustrate that PRD labor struggles are not limited to nationalist sentiment—providing a counterpoint to the resurgence of protectionist populism among workers in other countries, such as the United States.

There is another important feature of both the struggles documented in this book: the frequency of factory closures and relocations in the PRD, supplemented by some workers' awareness of earlier struggles (via word of mouth and, to some extent, the intervention of small, independent worker-support organizations), enabled workers to identify early warning signs and plan ahead. This shows a development of awareness, social networks, and organizational skills in contrast with the more spontaneous struggles typical of the 1990s and 2000s, but it may also mark the end of an era of regional development centered on labor-intensive manufacturing.

Labor Action or Class Action?

The PRD region has seen a few cases where labor struggles spread beyond the walls of one factory, neighborhood, or industry (such as the strike wave of 2010). But the two struggles documented in this book are more typical in their isolation and lack of solidarity from outside the workplace—despite the frequency of similar struggles in the surrounding area and time period.

The institutional context for this includes a series of labor regulations and laws issued by the Chinese state since the 1990s, encouraging workers to petition the state as an arbiter vis-à-vis private capital. These labor regulations may appear to protect workers' rights, but they are better understood as efforts to manage social conflicts between capital and labor within a predictable bureaucratic framework. "Rule of law" thus becomes not only a slogan of contemporary Chinese society but also a means of political legitimacy for the Chinese party-state. The promotion of law is a political device that safeguards a changing political regime in the process of privatization and liberalization, while also contributing to a rapid transfer of wealth and reconfiguration of social class and status.

The first and second generations of migrant workers in the PRD have accumulated experience, knowledge, and courage about how to alternately make use of, or defy, the state's regulations for their own interests. But while much academic literature on PRD labor struggles expresses optimism about this trajectory, the main author of this book urges a more sober assessment, at least for these two particular cases:

> Although workers' economic and political environment is constantly changing, there have been no significant changes in the form of labor struggles. Strikes continue to be spontaneous, and collective actions generally exhibit a low level of organization. Moreover, workers in general have not recognized the necessity and urgency of everyday organizing. Their consciousness has lagged behind changes in the conditions around them.

The structural weakness of workers vis-à-vis management is clear: the Chinese state has severely restricted collective labor rights, namely the right to organize and to strike, while local governments eagerly bid to secure production that they claim will assure jobs (even when that production is increasingly automated). Nevertheless, in both the workplace and the marketplace, migrant workers do possess structural and bargaining power. To date, this has been exercised primarily through wildcat strikes and riots, bypassing the official unions that serve the interests of management and the local state. Workers are sensitive to opportunities presented by the push of brands (such as Apple and other giants) to meet quotas for new models, so they have repeatedly come together at the dormitory, workshop, or factory level to voice demands in timely ways. They are also quick to leverage periodic labor shortage to boost wages, and have even scored a number of victories.

Although the development of an organized class movement is being restricted, factory-level strikes, collective bargaining over wages and social security, and petitions all attempt to wield power through collective action. In China's new industrial zones, the language of class is subsumed and collective actions still lack a formal political agenda working against the capital-state nexus, but this does not mean that "interest-based" collective actions might not eventually germinate into political actions in this rapidly shifting society. Despite the structural barriers, the new working class conjures up an array of everyday and collective forms of insurgency that threaten the forces of capital and thus require new forms of management by a state ever more anxious to subdue them—as illustrated by the de facto criminalization of collective labor actions since 2012, including the one-year detention of activist worker Mr. Wu discussed in this book, the December 2015 crackdown on multiple labor NGOs in the region, and the June 2016 arrest of bloggers Li Tingyu and Lu Yuyu.[4] Class opposition serves to reinforce collective identity and vice versa. In the cases presented in this book, we witness workers—motivated by desperation and the fear of losing everything when their factories relocate—becoming less atomized and developing ways of making decisions as they take part in collective action.

At a time when the labor movement is on the defensive worldwide, an impressive number of spontaneous protests and direct actions by workers have taken place in China. Deepened class conflicts are fueling labor insurgency in this still-crucial hub of transnational production. If the new generations of migrant workers succeed in building more militant networks beyond the present limits of individual workplaces, their struggles may well help to shape the future of labor and democracy not only in China but throughout the world.

Author's Preface
to the English Edition

As recounted in the introduction to the English edition of this book, the two labor struggles recounted in this volume took place during the third major sequence of widespread strikes in the PRD. The economic slowdown, in concert with government policies promoting industrial upgrade, was the main reason there were so many strikes centered on factory relocation at that time. In the case of City S described in the appendix, the government's factory relocation plan began in 2012 and ended in 2016. At the end of 2016, after many factories had relocated, this cycle of struggles was basically finished.

However, there are several points that must to be clarified. First, many industrial enterprises remain in the PRD. While large factories have left the industrial parks, many mainland Chinese bosses have opened small factories. Second, at the same time that factories have been leaving the PRD, some provinces in the interior of China have been reindustrializing. Complete deindustrialization was never in the interests of the bosses or the state. On the contrary, they wanted to maintain the complete industrial structure while developing additional high-end manufacturing techniques, such as automation, that would allow the entire industrial chain to compete with foreign capital.

Beginning in 2013, internal political battles among China's top-level rulers began to impact workers. In order to maintain stability over an extended period of economic adjustment, the state changed its attitude toward workers who fight for their rights. It has attacked all kinds of nongovernmental organizations (NGOs) that supported workers in such struggles, creating a range of obstacles to the expression of workers' demands.

Although workers' economic and political environment is constantly changing, there have been no significant changes in the form of labor struggles. Strikes continue to be spontaneous, and collective actions generally exhibit a low level of organization. Moreover, workers in general have not recognized the necessity and urgency of everyday organizing. Their consciousness has lagged behind changes in the conditions around them.

In order to get organized, it is essential to do preparatory work. On a fundamental level, Chinese workers are no different from those in the United States or any other country. We share a common fate and the common enemy of capitalism—sometimes manifested in the same transnational corporations and their supply chains, as exemplified by the suppliers of Walmart and Uniqlo featured in this book. Friends from other countries who are interested in the conditions and struggles of Chinese workers will most likely see from this small volume that, at present, Chinese workers have not yet organized to rise up against our own oppressors. We remain unable to determine whether we will be able to find a job or to keep it, like our fellow workers overseas with whom we are forced to compete for a shrinking supply of manufacturing jobs. Because we have not yet become organized, because we have not gathered our strength, and because we have not yet experienced serious battles, we know nothing about how such actions might be taken. China's new working class has only just been born. Due to its lack of history, traditions, and experience, it must study and continue to educate itself.

If this volume can help friends in other countries better understand the situation of Chinese workers and truly realize that there is no fundamental difference between workers in China and elsewhere, then it will have accomplished its goals.

Finally, I must thank all our friends who helped publish this work in English. Their enthusiastic support has made a valuable contribution by creating a dialogue between workers and their supporters in China and abroad.

Original Preface

The main factory relocation strike discussed in this book unfolded over the course of two weeks. The organizers had a set negotiation strategy, there were multiple clashes and negotiation sessions, and the methods employed by management and government offices to suppress the strike were quite complex. For these reasons, we felt compelled to carry out in-depth interviews in order to record the development of workers' struggles in the PRD.

We interviewed striking workers who held a range of positions at Factory D. There is an interview with workers' delegate Mr. Wu, who was the most active and was also persecuted the most severely. There are also interviews with people who served as organizers and the head negotiator, as well as with ordinary men and women from the factory who were more or less active in the strike.

Each person acted differently during the strike. Some became delegates (*gongren daibiao*), while others merely took part. There were both incidental factors and necessities that shaped these decisions. Individuals' actions were influenced by their work experience, number of years in the factory, family status, disposition, and even the specificities of their position in the factory. Ultimately, these actions determined the course of the strike.

These interviews record what various participants saw, heard, did, and thought during the strike. Mr. Wu's description is the most detailed. Although some portions of the accounts differ and other portions are repeated, we have faithfully recorded each account. This is because the impact of the strike was different for each participant. Each had a different understanding of the events and different attitudes toward them. From their various descriptions, we can understand the relationship between the delegates and the other workers. We see how each individual became involved in the strike and how each one viewed it. And we can also see how their different roles impacted the implementation of the strike, and how the strike changed the individuals involved.

It is never easy for workers to defend their rights, but as the economy has entered a new period of stagnation, it has become even more difficult. Some workers can't help thinking their lives are the hardest. They believe there's no solidarity among the workers, that the political environment they inhabit is the most toxic, and that workers from different eras or different countries would never face such challenges. But in fact, there are more labor disputes, particularly strikes, in this area than elsewhere (for example, in Taiwan workers rarely resist layoffs and wage cuts). As the first analysis in this collection states, "Ruthless conflict has yet to break out."

The [original] appendix, "Several Moments in the Struggle of Shanghai Workers 1939–1948," provides an initial point of reference. [In this English version, that appendix was replaced by a new one about another recent PRD factory relocation struggle.] What were the experiences of Shanghai workers before the 1960s and 1970s? What was the societal atmosphere at the time? What level of consciousness, organization, and conflict was there? It's not difficult to see that the struggle was fiercer and more brutal, and that the tribulations that workers went through were more severe. Still, the struggle itself is the same, and there are many points of commonality in the actions of workers, management, and the government.

Labor disputes continue unabated in the PRD. This small volume provides a reference for workers engaged in collective action, so that they can better navigate their own conflicts.

Analysis of a Typical Relocation Strike in 2013

Background

In 2005, the Guangdong government made a comprehensive plan to upgrade manufacturing in the PRD, and factory relocation was a key element of this plan. Amidst the shock of the 2008 global economic crisis, the provincial government began speeding up the implementation of economic adjustment policies and preparing for a major transfer of industry in 2012. At the end of 2011, the city of Shenzhen announced a detailed plan that would include the relocation of more than ten thousand enterprises within five years. Preparations at every government level were generally complete by 2012. In 2013, participating factories began to relocate under government leadership.

The economic upheaval continues to affect more and more enterprises. Many factories are adjusting their operations by moving to areas where wages are lower or where they can take advantage of incentives. For such factories, relocation is actively undertaken, a natural option that is not merely the passive implementation of government policy. Some relocating factories even receive support and subsidies provided by the government.

In the PRD, factory relocation has always been a major cause of labor disputes, and the wave of relocations in 2013 was accompanied by a large number of strikes. One focal point was the issue of economic compensation for laid-off workers.

Not every factory that relocated experienced strikes, nor was every strike severe. One female worker from a different PRD factory recalls: "When our factory relocated, the boss willingly compensated us. We were compensated for twelve months of work." Another female factory worker said:

> I know someone from my hometown.[5] When her factory was going to relocate, the boss said he wouldn't offer compensation. Then they blocked the gates and not two days later, the boss agreed to compensate them. I heard the boss already had the money ready. He hid it under his desk, and he wasn't going to give it to them unless they put up a fight.

Yet there were also many managers who, even if they were caught up on wage payments, were unwilling to spend a single penny compensating workers. They hated the way workers "get an inch and want to take a mile." In some cases, the more robust the enterprise, the less willing the manager was to give that inch. Their well-known sayings—"It's worth ten million yuan to break the workers," or, "I'd rather see the money in the river than in their hands"—enraged their employees and compelled them to take greater action.

So, why were the workers so set on getting this sum of money and how were they able to persevere for as long as they did?

First, an extended period of economic prosperity, increasing wages, and improving living conditions for the people of the PRD in recent years have bolstered the workers' demands. After the 2008 economic crisis, wage standards were frozen throughout the delta. The state undertook a far-reaching policy of economic stimulus, and, while there was a significant recovery for the profit margins of many enterprises, commodity prices also rose sharply. Base wages in the PRD have risen for the past five years, but each raise has been accompanied by an increase in rent and commodity prices.

In addition, tremendous industrial development in the

PRD over the past twenty-some years has created a new bourgeoisie and brought together a population of more than ten million workers, leading to countless labor disputes. Various experiences of collective and individual resistance, including work stoppages, road and factory entrance blockages, power cutoffs, complaints, arbitrations, media partnerships, and lawsuits, have also spread among the workers. This has given them a thorough understanding of the results of collective action, of the tactics employed by management and government organs, and of the relevant legal provisions (for example, that they can demand economic compensation when the labor contract is modified for purposes such as relocation). During a strike in 2013, a police officer said, "You workers are possessed! Whenever you start organizing, you call the police and seek out the government at the drop of a hat."

At the peak of the 2008 economic crisis, the workers were so beaten down that they could hardly lift their heads. However, just as one speeds up the pace after being forced to take a step backward, this period of setbacks increased the explosive power of later collective actions. After 2010, strikes demanding pay increases suddenly spread throughout the region. They were especially pronounced in the auto industry, such that bosses and the state became tense. Recalling a pay raise strike from four years before, a male car factory worker was moved to say:

> That felt like a whole different era. We went from getting a monthly pay increase of only ten yuan per year to a situation where, as soon as a strike began, people got a raise of seven or eight hundred yuan. How should I put it? Everyone was giddy and incredibly excited.

On the other hand, while workers gained some practical knowledge during these years, the economic boom accustomed them to an at-worst-I'll-find-a-different-factory attitude. Those who have not experienced bitter conflict generally lack the perseverance to resist. The bosses were also busy making money and did not see themselves as particularly hostile toward the strikers.

In addition to raising the minimum wage, government offices in the PRD carried out widespread interventions, arbitrating strikes in order to keep them from spreading. The state was not willing to bail out every boss, but in general it stood on the side of management. It placated, deceived, and oppressed workers. When necessary, it used force.

All these factors contributed to a climate in which the average strike was not particularly deep or far-reaching.

This sequence of factory relocation struggles has continued to the present. Some of them are long-lasting, with complex timelines and fierce conflict. Workers have tried all types of confrontation and are testing new methods.

A Brief Analysis of the Strike at Factory D

Strike Overview and the Impetus for Industrial Conflict

Factory D, located in a city in the PRD, was a well-established Hong Kong–owned manufacturer with a great deal of influence. In 2004, the boss made a lot of money and bought a piece of land in neighboring City Z to create a subsidiary plant. Operations at the old plant continued to decrease, but there were always sufficient orders. For some products that required sophisticated techniques, the company had to rely on the workers of the old factory. As a result, the workers were quite familiar with management changes in the enterprise.

Shortly after Factory D reopened after the New Year holiday in 2013, the boss planned to take the next step in merging the old factory with the subsidiary. Soon the entire factory went on strike, involving hundreds of workers, on the issue of relocation compensation.[6] The boss refused to give in, and the workers were not willing to give up. Over the course of twenty-some days, the workers "detained" the employer's vehicles three times, surrounded the office twice, held two sit-ins at the subdistrict government office, surrounded the labor station once, held two demonstrations near the factory, and marched to the municipal government to petition once. During the same period, the government called in the riot police four times and detained the workers en masse twice. Ultimately, the workers were "taught a lesson" (*xiuli*) [i.e. stopped and beaten by the police] on their way to the municipal government office. Some of the workers were detained for several days, and then the strike collapsed.

"Striking is hard. Even harder than working," said one middle-aged woman (*dajie*—literally, "elder sister"). Another was still restless and upset when she recalled what happened on the road to the government offices: "It's true. You didn't see it, but that day, they acted like bandits!"

The workers of Factory D were exhausted by their ongoing resistance. Ultimately, when confronted with the tremendous power of governmental organs, the nervous, excited workers suddenly came to their senses (*daxing*): lacking any ideas, they became scared and retreated.

The workers had never imagined the strike would take so long. One of the negotiating workers' delegates said they initially estimated the strike would last seven days at most. Many workers had heard of or witnessed strikes at other factories and had the impression that the matter would resolve itself in just a few days. Some workers said specifically that they didn't want to go into arbitration or a lawsuit because it would take too long. That is to say, they believed a strike would be much faster.

So, then, why did the boss and the workers fight for so long during this strike, and why was the conflict so fierce? One reason was the deep-seated resentment that both parties had built up.

The veteran workers of Factory D mentioned the boss's shady (*jianghu*) background and recalled how years ago he would patrol the shop floor and personally assault any workers who violated regulations. With the boss's approval, the guards were also aggressive and quick to become violent in those years. After 2006, the boss's younger brother, Boss Two, began assuming management of the factory. Although the incidents of violence decreased, the management began to "standardize" the factory. In the words of the workers, this meant a constant stream of new rules and fines. Like his elder brother, Boss Two liked to get into the thick of it. He even sniffed the shop floor's toilets to covertly apprehend workers who hid in the stalls to smoke. In 2007, the boss rescinded the perfect attendance bonus. In 2008, wages increased to 900 yuan per month, but meals were no longer included, and regardless of whether workers ate in the dining hall, they had to pay a dining fee of 270 yuan per month. In 2012, the annual bonuses were canceled.

Among relocation strikes in the PRD, workers erupting over long-accumulated grievances are common. For example, there was a Taiwanese-owned toy factory that had been in operation for twenty years. It had made a great deal of profit, and the boss owned a wide range of investments. The workers, however, spent years working in an environment full of toxic chemicals, which led to the death of at least five workers who truly paid with their lives. The employer was not the least bit interested in the diagnoses of the poisoned workers. In addition, this factory's overtime payments were structured illegally: the more units a worker finished, the less the worker was paid per unit. There was also a tragic scene in which two male workers who had worked too much overtime were unable to take a vacation and leapt to their deaths. In 2008, the toy manufacturer began to pay for pensions for a portion of the workers, but many workers were over the maximum age for buying into Social Insurance. Because they were afraid of losing their jobs, the older workers were usually quite cautious. Even if there was a strike, they would not dare stick their necks out, and they might not even take part. But when the factory was ready to relocate, the embittered older employees were not afraid to tear into the boss.

Aside from such grievances, the matter was compounded by the fact that some bosses were absolutely opposed to compensating workers and merely toyed with them. This also became an important factor in the continuation of the strike.

In the case of Factory D, the workers were certain that the boss had the funds to pay compensation. During the strike, the rumor that he was ready to spend ten million yuan just to swindle the workers made the group even angrier and increased their resolve to seek compensation.

This was not an isolated incident. In August 2013, a PRD textile factory decided to cut some departments. The owners announced they would rather "throw the money into the river" than compensate the workers. The latter responded with their own slogan, saying they would get the money "even if it meant draining the river dry."

Once the aforementioned Taiwanese-owned toy manufacturer had removed its machinery in May of 2013, a lawyer was sent to inform the workers, "As of today, the business has closed. Workers must apply for back wages today." Brimming with indignation, several hundred workers immediately marched to the district and municipal governments to seek an audience and were met on the highway by riot police.

Sometimes bosses put on a false air of conviviality that can be quite bewildering for the workers. In 2013 there were disputes over relocation compensation at a market-listed company in the PRD. Afterward, a male worker said:

> Once the strike started, the boss told us the factory wouldn't move for the next two years. She seemed sincere and appeared to be friendly, so we believed her. Who knew that afterwards they would continue to move one machine after another while we just grew more and more furious. In the end, she wouldn't put up the money and instead wanted to fight about it.

Such bosses, after pretending to be so considerate, suddenly turn around and refuse to acknowledge their debts. A foreman in Factory D said, "Workers are in the weaker position, they're the ones who are supposed to be slacking off. How does it end up that it's the boss who's taking it easy?" Leaving aside the question of whether or not workers are truly in the weaker position, the reason the bosses take it easy is because they know, "The factory is my property, and anything I say here goes. It's none of your business how much money I make and where I move the factory! Workers coming to me trying to get paid are just causing trouble." This is why the bosses do everything they can to get rid of the workers. The latter, on the other hand, believe that they need to settle up if the factory is going to move. It is these obdurate bosses who make the resulting conflicts more complicated.

Preparing for the Strike

The workers of Factory D began discussing relocation early on. The foremen discretely tracked changes in production, including changes in purchasing, the outsourcing of orders, and plans to relocate machinery. The foremen were trained interoperably and stayed attuned to the disclosures of veteran employees who were concerned about compensation issues. In this way, rights-defense (*weiquan*) circles emerged around each foreman.

The majority of workers at Factory D were unwilling to relocate with the factory, mainly because they didn't want to move. After living for a long time in one location, they had friends and relatives there and would have to start over if they moved. Even if offered a better position at the new factory with better pay, many would be unwilling to go. As for the managers, the branch factory had a completely new management structure. The old factory had an outdated management structure, so the managers were in an awkward position. Moreover, many of the managers had high wages and had spent many years in their positions, so their relocation compensation should have been significant. As a result, it was not at all strange that the managers planned to raise a ruckus (*naoshi*).

Once the boss had moved a few machines, the foremen held a small meeting, both to unify their demands and to decide when they would act. Everyone agreed they would begin the strike the next time a machine was loaded onto a truck. They would cut the power to every department so any uncommitted workers could leave the production line "with a clear conscience."

Not long after, the employees held an expanded meeting with lower-level managers. In order to maintain secrecy, the foremen invited only a few trusted workers to the meeting. Everyone was told, "Anyone who sticks their neck out and is ready to participate should come to the meeting." Based on reports submitted by certain managers at the meeting, they decided that three days later, when the owners were moving the injection-molding machine, they would block the truck and begin the strike. The group selected twenty people to serve as liaisons. These would be responsible for collecting "strike funds" to pay for drinking water and transport, and for coordinating the actions of each department.

Certain high-level managers at Factory D clearly knew that the workers were up to something, but they played dumb. Boss Two and his advisors remained in the dark, however — not because of the workers' secrecy, but due to Boss Two's hapless loss of support from the management. As a result, he was unable to deal with the "troublemakers." In some other factories, bosses who prepared in advance have had a much easier time relocating. One boss of a Hong Kong–owned factory forced his veteran employees and low-level management to resign while at the same time taking action vis-à-vis the middle and upper management. He compensated the managers who resigned and brought in new managers from other areas, ultimately ensuring that the factory could leave without compensating the employees.

At present, a significant number of factory relocation

strikes are instigated by low-level managers. Acting in their own interests, these managers are often more capable of standing up and fighting for their rights than workers. But once action has been taken, the low-level managers soon lose their resolve. They fear offending the boss and are accustomed to ordering the workers around. They hinder the further development of the strike because the considerations and actions of the workers do not benefit them.

The Workers' Determination in the Initial Period of the Strike

Not long after the second meeting, the management began to relocate machinery again. When an injection-molding machine had been moved onto a flatbed truck, a worker from the warehouse blocked the truck from leaving with a forklift. The strike had begun.

In the following days, both the employer and the government clearly underestimated the workers' resolve, believing the strike to be merely a perfunctory matter. Once the strike was in effect, the managers told everyone to return to work, but no one paid them any heed. Next, they brought out desks to have the workers sign resignations, collect their wages, and leave. Again, no one complied, save for a few casual workers (*linshigong*).[7] A police officer who claimed to represent the government arrived. Doing his best to intimidate the workers, he was instead surrounded by them and scolded until he took cover in an office building. Not long after, another officer came from the police station. He invoked his shared hometown with the workers' delegates, but they remained cold to him.

The next day, a dozen or so unidentified men came to the factory gate, loitered for some time, and then disappeared. It wasn't until the third day that the Big Boss showed his face. Before an assembly of all employees, he said they would not relocate and asked the workers to get back to work. A female worker said that no one believed him at that point. They shouted together, "You're treating us like three-year-olds!" When the Big Boss read how hostile the situation was, he turned and left.

Through the next few rounds of negotiations, the workers were united in their high spirits. Seeing their resolution, the bosses and the government were forced to take the strike seriously.

The owner and the workers held their first formal negotiation on the seventh day of the strike. The morning negotiations yielded no results, but the workers' delegates thought, "That's probably normal." In the afternoon, the owner suddenly changed his approach. Cameras had been set up in the negotiating room. When the workers' delegates entered, Boss Two took out a paper "notice" he had brought for the workers. It said the relocation had been canceled and warned the workers that they would be treated as absent if they did not return to work immediately. It also demanded that workers compensate the management for the losses accrued during the strike. The lawyers who had come to assist the workers took one look at the notice and left without saying another word. Later, the workers' delegates returned to the factory and explained the situation to the workers who were waiting for the results of the negotiations. Furious, the workers spontaneously poured out of the gates and blocked the road in front of the factory. They were quickly met by a great number of riot police who forced them to return to the factory. During the confrontation, one middle-aged female worker's arm was broken.

After this incident, there were several foremen who were no longer willing to serve as delegates. But the vast majority of workers were not only unafraid, they were even more incensed, and they immediately selected a new group of delegates. The next day, the workers gathered at the subdistrict office for a sit-in and demanded that the government intervene.

Soon the workers would face even greater trials.

Releasing the Truck and Blocking the Road

Everyone recalled that on the first day of the strike at Factory D, not only was the machinery not moved, but the flatbed truck the bosses had rented was forced to remain on the factory premises. Some said that the rent was five thousand yuan per day, others said it was nine thousand. In any case, the boss wanted the workers to release the truck as soon as possible. This was the first occasion when a significant conflict arose among the workers.

After the first round of negotiations broke down, the workers held a sit-in at the subdistrict government office, and the owner quickly agreed to a new round of negotiations. During the negotiations, the owner's lawyer spoke for him, saying he had agreed to pay compensation. The only remaining matter was agreeing on how much the compensation would be. The amount the lawyer proposed was three hundred yuan for each year that an employee had worked at the factory. After consulting with the boss, he increased it to four hundred, then five hundred, but it was still far removed from the workers' demands. Their delegates demanded two thousand yuan and had privately agreed they would go no lower than one thousand six hundred yuan. The lawyer said the boss had been forthright in agreeing to reopen negotiations, and that therefore the employees should be forthright in releasing the truck. To dispel the workers' concerns, the government officials also stepped in to guarantee the agreement. They promised they would help the workers and demanded that they release the truck. A dispute arose among the workers' delegates, but they quickly unified their position and agreed to release the truck. After negotiations concluded, the delegates reported on the progress that had been made and urged the other workers to release the truck. A dispute arose among the workers as well, but, other than complaining, those who did not agree did nothing to block the release of the vehicle. That evening, the truck that had been held on the factory premises for nine days was finally released.

Afterward, one delegate said that he supported releasing

the truck at that time mainly because the government had made written promises to help the workers and because he thought the workers ought to show good faith. There were also delegates, however, who did not consider the release an act of good faith and were instead concerned that the flagrant abduction of the truck would anger the government. They worried, "What will we do if the government doesn't help us?"

When the truck was released, there were only around a hundred workers on site. According to her recollection, one middle-aged female worker fell ill on the day of the negotiations and went home early. When she went back to the factory the next day, she discovered the truck was gone. Only when she anxiously asked her coworkers what had happened did she learn that it had already been released. She said that if she had been there, she would have lain on the ground to stop it from leaving.

Sure enough, the boss changed his tune as soon as the truck was released. When they resumed negotiations, only his lawyer attended. He changed his statement, saying the factory would not move, and asked the workers to return to work. The workers were extremely upset and some began to berate their delegates. A portion of them stayed to look after (*kanzhu*) the lawyer while a separate group of about a hundred went to surround the subdistrict office. Consequently, all of them were invited (*qing*) to the police station. They were held at a sports field detention center for several hours. Ultimately, they nabbed some to-go meals that the public safety bureau had bought for auxiliary police officers, which allowed them to relax a bit.

From then until the strike ultimately failed, the workers never saw the boss again. Later, some workers' delegates came to regret releasing the truck. But is it 100 percent certain that keeping the truck would have forced the boss to give in? Let us examine a separate strike.

One day in the winter of 2013, a PRD electronics factory was relocating when the workers went on strike to protest the boss's refusal to pay compensation. The striking workers blockaded the warehouse, stopping all the employer's shipments. In the middle of the second night, riot police suddenly attacked the nearly one hundred workers who were holed up in the factory. Many workers were beaten and knocked senseless, and many more were seized. Once the workers had been defeated, the employer began to ship his goods under the protection of the riot police. Still, the workers of the electronics factory refused to submit. On the next day, they gathered together to petition the city government, and the government department arranged for them to begin arbitration with the owner. The boss perfunctorily offered to hand out four hundred yuan per year of employment, then unilaterally ended the negotiations and demanded that the workers return to the factory and resume work. Meanwhile, the police continued to seize workers and went so far as to search the rooms they were renting. When the workers elected new delegates, their audience was "requested" by the government department, and they were forced to sign a document saying they would no longer participate in any collective action.

Based on this case, it is difficult to say whether the workers of Factory D would have been fixed up sooner if they had insisted on detaining the truck. The key question is not whether the workers employed a certain method of struggle, but whether they had a process for collective participation in the discussions of "should we do it or not," and "what should be done." For the workers of Factory D, the muddleheaded decision to release the truck certainly put them in a passive role. But if the group of workers who opposed releasing the truck had simply stopped it from being released, that would have been no less than an open admission to the bosses and government that there was internal strife. This, too, would have put them at a disadvantage. Suppose, on the other hand, that, before releasing the truck, everyone had openly discussed the proposition. At the very least, there would have been an opportunity for back-and-forth deliberations. This would have been far superior to hurriedly releasing the truck or directly exposing internal dissent.

If releasing the truck was the first major dispute within the group, the second major dispute revolved around whether or not to block the road.

Even on the first day of the strike, there were workers calling for the group to block the road and march to the government offices to seek an audience. According to the workers' delegates, there were workers calling for a road blockage almost every day, but the delegates told them they had to make their demonstrations reasonable and could not become over excited.

After the first breakdown in negotiations, the delegates were still able to restrain the workers. Though the workers who called daily for a movement onto the streets often said the delegates were "scared of a fight," the majority of workers were not influenced by this radical (*jijinpai*) faction.

The delegates' thinking about this was rather complex. They warned the workers that they must "protest rationally," but internally they discussed an incident they had seen in which workers from another factory completely blocked a main road until "cars were backed up from the intersection all the way to Wanlian Mall." This blockade had compelled the boss to agree immediately to the workers' demand for compensation.

In the end, the delegates feared they would be charged with inciting the workers to disrupt public order, but personally they knew well that if the workers didn't disrupt (*nao*) anything, they would have no hope of drawing a single penny from the boss, no matter how eloquently the delegates spoke on their behalf.

Looking back, one delegate said, "It was only on the last day when the workers took action that the delegates lost control."

"The last day" was the day the workers collectively marched to the municipal government to seek an audience. After walking more than three hours, they came to a secluded part of the road where they were attacked by riot police and detained. That was the day the strike was lost. As far as the control (*chengkong*) goes, that does not mean that all of the unrest caused by the workers was planned in secret by their delegates. Above and beyond the dictates of the delegates, workers undertook radical (*guoji*) actions that the delegates never participated in. However, the delegates were summarily judged and bore the consequences for the workers' "ruckus." On the last day of the strike, someone yelled, "C'mon, let's have dinner at the municipal government." When the workers asked that the delegates go with them, those who foresaw a bleak outcome left. One delegate warned, "There may not be any dinner if you go now." Another delegate said later that he had asked the workers to line up in teams of five and march forward in unison. He said if they would do that he would go with them. Of course, this may just have been an excuse to bow out.

PRD workers are always eager to block the roads because they've learned from experience that blocking roads produces swift results. Moreover, there are generally no punishments for doing so.

One worker recalls that when they went on strike and visited the labor station, an employee who was surrounded by workers said, "Okay! Okay! We've said we'll help you resolve it. If it doesn't get resolved, just go ahead and do whatever you like. Block the road, petition, whatever you want."

Another worker remembered a different strike in which a police officer told them, "Just don't block the whole road. Block half, and there won't be any problem."

But when the strikers at Factory D went to the subdistrict office for a sit-in, everyone there received two text messages from the government on their phones. The first was a provision from the *Petitioning Regulations*. The second said, "Let's not block the road here or elsewhere. It's said we'll be detained for five to ten days." But many of the workers were unfazed by the prospect of being detained for a few nights and did not take it seriously.

However, the workers' prediction that "blocking the road won't be a problem" fell through. The terror of being beaten on the last day and the punishments handed down afterward exceeded the workers' expectations.

The Emergence, Oversight, and Protection of Workers' Delegates

An important step in the organization of any strike is the emergence of workers' delegates. In many PRD strikes, the emergence of delegates is quite simple.

For example, in a 2014 strike in a Korean-owned PRD factory, a Korean manager struck a female foreman. When news of the incident reached the shop floor, a middle-aged male worker yelled, "We don't even have basic human rights! Everyone stop working!" The workers stopped work and gathered in the factory's central area. The boss came out and apologized, but he did not mention any of the issues surrounding wages. Dissatisfied, the workers surged out of the factory gates and blocked the road. Before long, the police brought two *jixundui*[8] vans to the scene and asked the workers' delegates to come forward and negotiate. Everyone naturally focused on the middle-aged worker who had initiated the strike—the first workers' delegate was chosen.

So how were the delegates at Factory D generated? After the strike began, the owners and government offices were constantly calling on the workers to elect delegates. The workers insisted that there were none and that each individual could represent only himself or herself. In truth, the workers had selected delegates on the afternoon that the strike began. The process was quite simple. Everyone gathered at a certain location in the factory and several foremen stood together in front of everyone. Someone said loudly, "They will be the delegates. Does everyone agree?" and they were unanimously approved. The whole process took only a few minutes.

The foremen of Factory D prepared for the strike and served as delegates, but they told the workers, "[If the government asks you,] don't tell anyone who the delegates are.

Say we're all representing ourselves." When the Labor Bureau asked the workers to elect delegates that would negotiate with the owners, the workers gave various excuses. Several women recalled, "[The government] asked us to elect delegates and we said, 'We wouldn't dare elect delegates. If they get bought out, what would we do? The delegates would take the cash and run off, and then what could we do?'"

The workers' delegates were unwilling to be seen by the owners and government as those that were leading the resistance. They preferred to act as if they were hapless individuals who had been forced to step forward by the other workers. In fact, the delegates were so afraid of reprisals from the boss that they agreed among themselves to rent a car. On the day of compensation, the delegates would be compensated first. They would then wait until everyone had gotten their money, and the rented car would ensure that that they could drive off and escape. This somewhat naive strategy was of no use because, in the end, the one attacking them was the government.

The workers understood the concerns of their delegates, but they also had their own concerns, for they knew full well that more than a few strikes fail when the workers' delegates are paid off. The women workers were always eager to recount stories from their hometown, and this was no exception. One said, "A hometown friend of mine was in a strike where several of the workers' delegates took the boss's money and ran off. The other workers didn't know what to do, and in the end, they didn't get a single cent!"

Concerns continued to build. The workers didn't want to supervise their delegates, but they also didn't know what they would do if the delegates ran off. At the same time, the workers were not really thinking about how to protect their delegates.

During the strike at Factory D, the workers who were constantly calling for a road blockage berated their delegates for being too timid. On the last day of the strike, they said the delegates were "afraid for their lives." Some female workers stood at the gate and loudly chastised them as "traitors" who "had yet to lose any of their own money." Unfortunately, these women never considered how they would defend the delegates if they were truly going to be detained. This point became extremely obvious after the strike failed. A strike may have many activists, but once the workers' delegates are detained, many workers get scared, take the money, and go. Another active participant in the strike said remorsefully:

> We still regret it. We really shouldn't have marched on the road to the municipal government at that point. He [Mr. Wu, who was detained that day] got hurt. But we had gone out twice before without anyone stopping us, so we thought no one would stop us this time. One time we went out from the gate and blocked the road for more than ten minutes, and the other time we took a banner and circled the factory. No one stopped us either time, so we had no idea they would seize us the third time. . . . It was the government that made us elect those delegates, and then they seized them.

Most of the workers were released the day after they were seized. Some of them were so shaken up that they ran off without even asking for their wages. Other workers thought that so long as there was no one causing a stir, everyone would be released soon. The delegates had not been seized, but they were hiding and no one was organizing the strike. The result was that, within a few days, the workers of Factory D were unable to sustain their collective struggle.

Taking advantage of this breakdown among the workers, the boss immediately announced that all the workers' delegates had been fired. At the same time, he "invited" the other workers to resume their positions at the factory. For those who refused to come back, the boss was still willing to pay the symbolic severance pay of four hundred yuan for each year worked. The workers helplessly accepted this result. However, what the workers did not expect was that the most active delegate, Mr.

Wu, would be held for one year and nine days.

Among recent strikes in coastal areas, the punishment of one year and nine days set a new record. After being released, Mr. Wu began to reflect on the issue of protecting delegates. He thinks that the main role for workers' delegates should be to transmit the opinions of the workers to the owners and the government. A delegate is not an organizer. He or she holds a role different from that of a labor leader (*gongren lingxiu*). A labor leader can encourage, network, and even forge alliances between different factories, so "they have a 100 percent chance of meeting with repression." Naturally, he believes that this kind of labor leader does not currently exist.

However, in the case of Factory D, it was the foremen who initially worked to organize and network. The first delegates were chosen from among this group, so these were not simply negotiating delegates. In other words, they did indeed act as "labor leaders" throughout this struggle. Moreover, the workers' delegates were not recording devices that could mechanically recite the demands of the workers. Once the collective rights defense reaches a certain stage, so long as the workers are unwilling to submit, they have no choice but to strengthen their organization. No matter whether they're called workers' delegates, negotiating delegates, or activists (*jijifenzi*), they must take on the task of organizing or there will be no way to sustain the strike through ongoing negotiations. Even if the delegates steadfastly obey the law and constantly express their goodwill to the bosses and the government, so long as they are unwilling to sell out the workers, it will be hard for these forces not to see them as a nuisance.

Different Approaches of the Workers during the Strike

As described above, from start to finish, Mr. Wu played an active role. On the last day, when the women preparing to go to the government office were trying to badger "those people" (the delegates) into coming with them, the foremen urged Mr. Wu not to go. Mr. Wu said that at the time he was worried (about repression), but seeing all his coworkers so agitated, he felt it was his responsibility to go with them. Later, on the road to the government offices, a uniformed police officer pointed at Mr. Wu and shouted, "Quick! It's him!" Immediately, a group of "black clad" (*heipi*) officers rushed forward. Though the scene was terrifying for the workers, those female workers who had just scolded Mr. Wu surrounded him and tried to stop the police from seizing him.

It's well known that during collective struggle, women often rush to the front lines. Describing the behavior of such "girls" during the collective action, one male factory worker said, "When we had to fight the government, the girls pushed to the very front. The day we went to the city and people were beaten and detained, it was always the women who were leading us. We all said, "The men are like women nowadays. They even rely on the women to fight and get thrown in jail. They let the women face off against the riot police."

To this day, PRD workers fighting for their rights never intend to fight the government. Still, many are prepared to suffer a beating. During strikes, female workers often charge up to the front lines in the hope of mitigating the state's violence. In times like these, it isn't necessarily out of fear that male workers stay in the back. Rather, the workers collectively recognize that male workers in the front are more likely to be beaten, and that as soon as the front lines are broken, it becomes difficult for those behind them to persevere.

When discussing the female workers in this strike, one workers' delegate commented that those uncultured women offered little assistance, save for their love of conflict. But in fact, it was these female workers' instinctive impetuosity that helped the strike to develop. Some workers' delegates, in contrast, shrank back when there were twists and turns in the development of the strike.

Many people were afraid, but there were also fearless

workers who came forward. After the first breakdown in negotiations, one male worker stepped forward to serve as a delegate. He was originally a senior chef in the factory's cafeteria, so many workers knew him. When the cafeteria was outsourced, he was transferred to a packaging machine. He did not participate in the first few days of the strike, but when he saw that some workers' delegates had resigned following the breakdown of negotiations, he came forward and asked to be a delegate, saying, "I'm not afraid."

There was also a middle-aged male worker who was active from beginning to end despite not being a delegate. He pushed to the front during every collective action. On the last day, for being part of the team carrying the banner, he was struck to the ground and imprisoned for more than a week. After his release, there was no one organizing anymore, and he didn't know what to do. Otherwise, "I would have kept it up if someone was organizing it." Reflecting on his behavior during the strike, he felt he acted "like a club," attacking wherever the delegates told him to.

Just as there were active participants, there were, of course, inactive ones. When the strike was called, some workers looked for new jobs and did not participate in the collective action in any way. The active participants also saw their enthusiasm wane. Mr. Wu said that in the first few days, every delegate attended every meeting. Later, they began to slack off, and it was impossible to assemble everyone.

The Government's Attitude

The measures employed by the government are the best evidence of the government's attitude toward the strike. In a situation where the boss was refusing to give any ground, the actions taken by the government made clear where it stood.

Generally speaking, the government does everything it can to suppress the workers so the boss can save money and relocate easily. In some cases, the government uses various methods against "ungrateful" (*buzhihaodai*) workers who have become accustomed to obtaining raises and compensation in recent years. These include procrastination, deception, intimidation, induced arbitration, and deterrence by force. If the workers still refuse to give in, the government becomes irritated and bares its fangs to bite the workers. Still, they are very measured; they don't want the workers to gain more accolades by causing a stir without consequences, nor do they want to push the workers to the point of desperation.

In the electronics factory mentioned above, the workers occupied the factory for only one day before being attacked, while those from Factory D managed to raise a ruckus for more than two weeks before meeting with suppression. The workers at a sheet metal plant agitated intermittently from January until August. After encountering a setback during a visit to the municipal government, they returned to the factory only to be met by gangsters (*heishehui*) who had been stationed there. After this staggering defeat, they were forced to sign resignations. How does the government select the moment to employ "the ultimate measure" (*zuihou chushou*) in different strikes? We do not know. But one thing is worth emphasizing: the government does not stand in the service of any individual capitalist. Instead, it attempts to take a higher position governing the entire system of class rule. In considering how to respond to the present sequence of relocation strikes, the government triages in order to avoid acting hastily and becoming enmeshed in multiple conflicts.

After the workers of Factory D went on strike, a man in a police uniform came to intimidate them. Subsequently, a different officer expressed friendship with the workers. When neither of these methods worked, they began to delay. Personnel from the labor station and the police station came every day to inspect the factory. Seeing that the workers were responsibly occupying the factory, they praised the "reasonable demonstrations" of the workers and promised to help them resolve the issue. But the workers were not fools. They weren't striking just so they could sit there and listen to praise from the government. No one took these visitors too seriously, and they became irritated when forced to listen to them at length.

On the afternoon of the first negotiation, the boss and the government were obviously singing the same tune. The boss denied that he was moving the factory, and the government denied that the factory had undertaken any illegal actions. It is possible that they expected the workers to leave the factory gates that day, because the riot police arrived on the scene almost immediately. Yet the first large-scale use of police force cannot be considered to have been in earnest—it was only to push the workers back onto the factory grounds. Unfazed, workers returned to the factory and confined Boss Two in the office building for nearly two hours.

During the second negotiation, the Labor Bureau made written commitments and demanded that the workers release the truck, but the boss did not show his face until the third negotiation. The low-level government employees even complained to the workers, "Your boss is shameless. We'll drive him away sooner or later." It is impossible to know whether the boss deceived even these government employees. But the workers noted that regardless of whether the low-level government personnel were dissatisfied with the boss, the government never forced him to return to the table. In matters of profit, the government stood with the bosses from beginning to end.

The government is a mighty entity and has long prepared a set of methods for dealing with workers who fight for their rights. During the 2013 sequence of relocation strikes, the government often intervened—first to suppress the workers, forcing them to tighten their belts and thereby helping the bosses weather the economic winter, and second to maintain state control of the situation. They did not allow individual bosses to arbitrarily handle labor disputes, nor did they have any intention of abandoning the position of foremost arbitrator. Another point that is clear is that in handling this sequence of factory relocation strikes, state actors didn't actually reveal their full strength. Because workers lightheartedly took part in the strikes and because their level of organization, will to resist, and experience were all lacking, the state did not need to wantonly suppress them. It just needed to make a few perfunctory moves, waver a bit, delay some more, perform a few crackdowns, and then roll out again, and the whole matter was resolved.

Conclusion

How have the workers of Factory D fared since the strike? Some have taken positions at other factories, while others are working part time for friends with small businesses. Some have returned home for the time being; others have taken a few months off and are in no hurry to find work, while still others are trying to start their own businesses. In general, the workers have not simply fallen on hard times. Ultimately, good work is hard to find and rotten work is common. But over the previous few years, the workers' families had been able to build up some savings.

In recent years, China's capitalist economy has been in a state of constant adjustment in hopes of pulling it out of the recession faster. This sequence of factory relocation strikes was the instinctual response of PRD workers to these adjustments. That the strikes have continued for years is just a matter of fact, and few clear organizational traits have been established. There has been almost no self-conscious synthesis of the methods employed by striking workers, such as road blockages and collective meetings with the authorities, much less any intentional development of these methods.

As a whole, the region's workers are not afraid to strike. When necessary, they are even ready to break the law by blocking roads, stopping shipments, and petitioning the government en masse. If a method is useful, the workers will employ it. If not, the method is temporarily shelved. When they are beaten or seized, the workers face a period of fear marked by moments of fury. When it is all over, they will not discuss the terror they felt, nor will they mention the intense hatred they harbor for the bosses.

Whether in relocation strikes or other types of labor disputes, workers are more conscious than they once were of the legality of their actions. Once they begin to mobilize, however, they will not hold the law as something holy and inviolable. So long as they believe an action will achieve the goal of defending their rights, they are willing to try it. One could say that workers now hold the contradictory psychology of being unwilling but unafraid to break the law. This is not at all strange. Simply pull any article, and you'll see that, in the past twenty years, innumerable PRD strikes have violated any number of laws (for example, destroying productive facilities, damaging property, disturbing public order, inciting unrest). But until now, the state has never implemented such a wide range of repressive methods on such a large scale. As for why this cage was opened, it can only be because the high level of prosperity has established making money as the top priority for both bosses and the state, with the assumption that everything else can wait. What's more, given the contradictory state of labor relations, the meticulous application of repressive mechanisms against such spontaneous strikes can, in fact, provoke the workers, making matters more complex. The government is well aware of this.

Having passed through a lengthy battle for survival, the workers of the PRD have dug in their heels. They have more confidence and greater demands. They want to achieve more, yet management is more firmly set against them than in past years. The state is armed to the teeth and will intervene on a moment's notice to protect the overall interests of the capitalist class, but it also does not intend to bruise the workers so badly that they dare not speak again. Serious battles have not yet broken out. In the coming period of collective struggles, will there be a swell of activists (*jijifenzi*) who view workers' interests through the lens of class? Will the most prescient segments of the workers learn how to resist the demands of the bosses? Will workers and their delegates become more tightly knit through such collective actions? In short, will the workers of the Pearl River Delta take the next step forward? We must wait and see.

Oral Histories of the Strike

Delegate Wu

"Circles formed in each department as workers began communicating with one another."

The Basic Situation in the Factory

Living and Working Conditions

In 2004, I got my start at this factory when it posted a help-wanted sign on the gates. Temporary residence permits could be obtained through the factory, but the workers had to pay for them and there were no wage advances given. The workers' wages were also held for two months. The factory had ample supply and there was enough work for two shifts per day. We worked overtime every day except Sunday, and there were basically no breaks. It was exhausting. Not working overtime was considered absenteeism. Unless one had an excuse, one would not receive that day's wages and would also be fined three days' pay. When there was a rush order, we worked through the night. We had time off during power staggering,[9] but we weren't paid for those days. Taking time off usually required approval from several people, including the foreman and supervisor.

My wife and I were both working at the factory. We ate and lived together, took care of one another. We weren't thinking about the working conditions at the time.

I was assigned to the cutting department where we made picture frames and stands. There were more than fifty people in the department, with around ten additional helpers (*zagong*). We were responsible for coding and inspecting the materials, and also for tallying, adjusting the machinery, quality control, and repairs.

The foremen were given the orders every two weeks. We would see what was urgent and do those tasks first. The management said we were paid a piece rate, but actually we were paid according to a combination of hours worked and items completed. Basic production quantities were set in the factory and there was a standard price list, but the work had to be completed in the set time period or our pay would be deducted. How much you worked depended on whether the work assigned to you was easy or not. That depended on your connections—there was clearly preferential treatment for some. When good materials were put through the machine, they came out in many well-formed pieces. That was a little faster, so the pay was higher. Other materials were wide in some places and narrow in others. They had to be put through many times and then trimmed. For the same amount of work, fewer goods were produced, resulting in lower pay. The production quotas were just rough estimates. The materials were pretty rough at the start. Then we would dice them into flat square sheets.

The boss set the unit prices arbitrarily, without considering production quantity. But the unit price was a sham because the underlying principle was that pay could not exceed sixty yuan per day. Monthly pay came to seven hundred or eight hundred yuan, with no more than twenty or thirty yuan difference among the workers. (Nearby factories all had comparable pay.)

The piecework income for our line was averaged for each worker. A portion of their pay was given to the helpers. Their pay was taken directly from our piecework earnings because the boss didn't pay them a separate wage.

On the shop floor, everyone brought their relatives with them. The managers gave their own people the tallying (*jishu*) and master craftsmen (*shifu*) positions. There was a supervisor and an assistant manager who were both from Sichuan. They were relatives because one had married the other's sister. That assistant manager had all the piecework, quality control, and coding done by relatives. No one could fight them and win. Those doing quality control and piecework earned a few hundred more per month than we did. Two mechanics with connections did hardly anything at all. They just sat in the office drinking tea and chatting. Usually when I was processing the materials, there was nothing I needed to speak to the mechanics about. All you needed to know was how to use a tape measure and how to adjust equipment — something you could learn in half a day. The people who were being taken care of could go home early. They could just go home after their quota was completed and didn't have to do the four hours of overtime. But there were only a few people who got that kind of treatment. Among the workers, it was common for cliques to form.

In the past we got year-end bonuses: a hundred yuan for every year worked, with an upper limit of six hundred yuan. Then, in 2008, we didn't receive a year-end bonus, and after 2010 the bonuses stopped altogether. Workers objected at the time, but no one raised a fuss. The year-end bonuses weren't written into the contracts, so if the boss decided not to pay them, he wasn't breaking the law.

Workers were fined if they failed to clock in. Those who damaged the materials they were working on were generally not fined because it usually went unreported. If it were reported, it would make things difficult for the management, so it was simply handled on the shop floor.

During rush jobs, the management would bring in people of the Yi ethnic minority from Liangshan for a few months. These workers were paid less and also had to give a portion of their wages to their own boss (*lingtou*). The Yi boss hired his own relatives and oversaw them in the factory. They were spread among the various departments. The young ones spoke decent Mandarin, but not the older ones, who hadn't attended school. If one of these Yi workers wanted time off, they had to seek approval from both the factory management and their own boss. The factory would give their wages to the Yi boss, who would then distribute them. Their hourly wages were one or two yuan less than ours.

Our factory supplied goods to Walmart. Every year when Walmart came to inspect the factory, the management taught us how to answer their questions. If we were surveyed and answered correctly, we got two hundred yuan. I was never surveyed. In the beginning, the factory hired child workers every year for every department. The child workers were younger than sixteen years old, usually around fifteen. They came from all over, including Yi people from Sichuan. When the factory was being inspected, they would make the child workers leave. They told them not to come in.

In 2007, the furniture department was standardized (*zhengguihua*) and split into three or four departments. We had one day off per week and were paid by the hour. Usually we wouldn't work overtime, but if we were working on a rush job, we would do four hours of overtime at a standard overtime rate. The other several departments in the factory moved to the new system and the basic wage was raised slightly. I believe everyone's wages were increased. The workers were delighted.

Mechanics generally oversaw the shop floor and were responsible for two machines each. They got 1,140 yuan per month, including a bonus for skilled workers (*jishu jintie*) of around three hundred yuan. We were paid according to the roster and would punch in directly after signing our names.

Some time later, I began working as a mechanic and became close with the foremen. Sometimes we drank together—everyone would put in twenty or thirty yuan, and it deepened our camaraderie. I personally have a strong sense of responsibility, so I worked earnestly to maintain the machines and decrease waste.

A separate engineering department was responsible for maintaining the machines. The repairmen in the engineering department were earning four or five thousand yuan per month and could fix the large cutting benches (*pingbanji*).

Our factory's busy season was generally from June to October, when we worked four hours overtime every day and sometimes through the night. The other seasons were slower. Usually if we worked overtime we earned around seventeen hundred yuan. The mechanics had to work overtime, too. I never thought of leaving the factory. I had an extra allowance, it was laid back, and I got along well with my coworkers, so I had no desire to leave. All of the managers in the furniture department had come as a complete team from a bankrupt furniture factory in Dongguan, so there was no chance I would get a job in management.

Management

The Big Boss came to mainland China in the 1990s and opened the factory. I heard that his family originally escaped to Hong Kong during the Cultural Revolution. When he came back to invest, he was fifty or sixty years old. He had a wife but no children, and he rarely showed his face. He liked to party so he held galas for New Year celebrations and invited bands to perform for Mid-Autumn Festival. In 2006, he went to Huizhou and handed this factory off to his younger brother ("Boss Two") to manage. There were very few managers from Hong Kong, and they were all in senior management.

Boss Two never cast a friendly smile upon the workers. If workers smoked in the factory, they were fined two hundred yuan and forbidden from working overtime for the next two weeks. Every year several workers had the bad luck of being caught. There were surveillance cameras in the factory, mainly to monitor whether we were working or chatting.

The managers in the factory were usually cultivated internally. My cousin was a common worker (*pugong*)[10] at first, but he began getting together with the supervisor to play mahjong, have drinks together, even inviting him over for dinner to eat

a freshly slaughtered chicken. That was how he became a foreman. All foremen had a small office and a wage that was one or
two hundred yuan per month higher. Above the foremen were
the assistants, supervisors, and directors.

Social Insurance and Occupational Injuries

Social Insurance[11] was purchased voluntarily. Those who didn't
buy it signed to opt out of the programs. Only two or three workers in a hundred bought pensions. Most managers didn't buy them
either. People said if they worked for only a short time, they'd still
have to keep paying for it for years, and who could afford that?

The management forced us to buy work-related injury insurance. When workers started working at the factory, they
had to have their blood drawn, and every year they had to pay
a thirty-five-yuan testing fee. But the management never gave
the test results to the employees. Instead, they gave us certif-
icates of health. The money they collected was real, but the
tests were fake. In our cutting department, the machines were
equipped with saw blades. If workers were careless while feeding materials into the machine, they would injure their hands,
sometimes losing a finger. There were many incidents like this;
it happened every year. While in the hospital we would receive
our base wage and a living-expenses fee of twelve yuan per day.
When I was injured, they didn't give me my technical allowance, just my base wage. There were many workers from other
factories in the hospital ward with me whose bosses didn't care
for them at all. I thought I was pretty lucky to have my medical
expenses reimbursed.

There was a lot of turnover in the factory, so they were
seeking new employees all through the year. The work was
labor intensive, but it was not technically demanding. All it
required was a little training. Still, young people didn't last.
The work environment was pretty bad. The injection-molding
machine was hot and using the cutting machine created a great
deal of dust. Every day we had to change our face masks several

times, but the young people couldn't get used to wearing them. Usually workers didn't ask for the masks, and the managers wouldn't actively hand them out. We had to wear earplugs, but young workers couldn't get used to those either and refused to wear them. We used Xylene on the shop floor, so ventilation and face masks were required. But the workers had a poor sense of self-preservation. When I told them about the risks, they thought I was exaggerating. Many people injured their fingers on the job, but more serious accidents were rare.

Environment, Food, and Welfare

Some workers rented rooms in a corrugated iron building outside the factory for fifty yuan per month. In those days, there were many housing units with metal siding. They were noisy and hot. The first apartment I rented cost 170 yuan per month. It was a lot. There were few hostels back then, and when I went out on Saturday and Sunday to look for a place, it was already too late. Nothing was open. There was nowhere to play mahjong, but there were lots of video halls.

In the past, there was no wage deduction for eating in the cafeteria. The food was nothing much. They just served tofu and tofu skin. The pumpkins and winter melons weren't even peeled, and there were grains of sand and cockroaches in the food. The meat in the dishes had been beaten with a machine until it was pulped. We joked that it had been turned into meat molecules. But it was free, so we still ate it. They started charging a dining fee in 2008. They wanted the workers to sign their names, and many were unwilling to sign. The managers first got their relatives to sign, then said we would have to collect our pay and leave if we didn't sign. A small number of people refused to sign and left. I signed because my wife had gone back to our hometown, and I was too lazy to cook.

Originally, our factory also provided a few extra perks (*fuli*): a small bag of laundry detergent and two rolls of toilet paper once per month, and some fruit every Monday. Later,

Boss Two's secretary canceled all of that.

From 2004 to 2005, there were more than two thousand people in the factory. There was a drawing at the New Year banquet that only those who had been there for two years could participate in. The awards were a color television set, a bicycle, and a cellphone. They were gifts sent by the suppliers. After 2006, there were no more New Year banquets.

Security

In the past, there was an incident at our factory almost every month. They're all registered at the police department.

I heard that when the boss was young, he had a violent streak. In those days, the factory had its own riot squad (*fangbaodui*) in addition to the security guards. The employees who took part got an extra one hundred yuan per month and were armed with a steel pipe. If a fight broke out in the factory, the riot squad had to preserve order.

I once got into a fight with a guard. We were getting off work and I was exhausted. After we'd lined up to clock out, someone cut the line. It was chaotic. A young guard immediately jumped on a desk to scold people. I said, "Who the hell are you yelling at? Who in here isn't your uncle or your aunt?" He was going to hit me, but we had more people and pinned him down.

When the guards beat people, some were purposefully finding fault with someone and some were helping their friends to pick a fight. There were fights between managers, too, and between managers and workers. Guards also fought with managers, but in general, most incidents involved guards beating workers.

Twice the factory's head of security was attacked. The first time, people were playing mahjong in the street outside the factory on the night before Chinese New Year when several people from Hunan decided to come in and make trouble for the manager. The head of security showed up to intervene and was struck in the head by a brick. The second time was for a dispute in the factory among people from Anhui. The head of security was also from Anhui, and when he came out to intervene, someone from his hometown cut his leg three or four times with a knife.

One security guard was the head of security's brother. It was crowded during lunch one day and this guard's wife said that a worker from Guizhou had grabbed her butt. When the guard heard this, he went to look for that worker from Guizhou. A factory manager from Guizhou came out to speak on the worker's behalf. When he said the guard had no proof, several guards beat the two of them so badly they were hospitalized. The boss compensated them, and the manager lost face and left.

In 2008, all the guards in the factory were replaced and the head of security also left. The management no longer allowed the head of security to directly hire people, because the former heads had only hired their own relatives. Initially, the head of security had reported directly to the boss. Later, it was changed to the administration department. The guards became more honest, and there were no more incidents of fighting.

From 2006 to 2013, they were constantly moving the factory's machinery to Huizhou. They would move one machine today and the next one tomorrow. When they opened the branch in Huizhou in 2006, the more than one thousand workers at the old location were gradually decreased to around three hundred.

Due to the 2008 financial crisis, we took the Chinese New Year holiday early. There was a long period without overtime work, and sometimes there was nothing to do. We swept the floor, did odd jobs, and hung out in the factory to get our base wage.

The First Relocation in 2006

In 2004, the boss bought a plot of land in Huizhou and built a factory there. He had the first batch of machines moved in 2006.

Without asking any of the workers if they were willing to relocate, he asked workers who lived offsite to bring their luggage, get on a bus, and go. No one from the cutting department went. We surrounded the office and asked the manager if the boss meant that the entire factory was relocating. The manager said that was right and announced that the workers who were unwilling to go would have a one-month vacation because all the machines had been packed up.

At the time, we knew absolutely nothing about the laws and regulations. Thirty workers from our department went to the township labor station. The workers who were calling the shots were those who were assertive and spoke openly. The Labor Bureau personnel first urged us to move to Huizhou. Later, they signed promises to come to the factory and help us resolve the issue. Two or three of them came. They went into the boss's office, and when they came out they said he wasn't there. They told us to wait patiently for several days and trust the government. At the time, we didn't know there was such a thing as relocation compensation. We just wanted to get our wages, but the boss was demanding that we move to Huizhou with him.

As more departments relocated, our numbers grew. Everyone waited in the factory for about two weeks, watching as the machines were relocated. Sometimes we went to the Labor Bureau together. Everyone was worried we wouldn't be paid, and the managers completely ignored us. No one made a stir at the time. We were quiet, and some of us had already begun to look for new jobs. The personnel from the Labor Bureau came once more. When they were done talking to the boss, they came out and asked for workers' delegates to go in. While the members of the Labor Bureau were there, the boss asked the employees to write resignations. Those who did were compensated and left. Four or five delegates went in, including myself. Some of my coworkers asked me to go because I was relatively active.

Of the fifty workers in the cutting department, more than twenty went to Huizhou. In the end, there were only five of us left. The boss spoke separately to each department, and the discussions were on different days. Each department relocated separately, so the workers were dispersed and unable to make unified demands. At the time, we didn't understand how all the departments related to one another. Everyone was just looking out for themselves.

In truth, the boss had decided much earlier that he would open a furniture department in our factory, though he told no one. As the factory was relocating, the boss simply found some workers from a furniture factory in another city to come work at ours. They didn't know what was going on. When almost all the positions had been filled, the boss said the furniture department needed people and asked us to stay. The new factory in Huizhou was in a remote location and hiring was difficult there, so those who went to Huizhou regretted it. They became resentful, feeling the boss had swindled them. They were irritated, but they didn't know at which point they had been swindled or how they could vent their anger. There was no use in filing a complaint with the government—no one would help us.

The newly established furniture department produced jewelry cabinets for export. I still worked in the cutting department, and later I worked as a mechanic, for which I received an additional technical allowance. Around that time, there was another furniture factory in Dongguan whose boss had fled, and the workers had blocked the road for three days demanding their pay. The township government responded by selling the factory and machines to pay the workers. Our boss knew a manager there, and he had him bring all the workers to our factory. Some of them had already found new jobs, but our boss asked them to quit and come work for him immediately, saying he would give them two months' pay. He also bought a whole set of new machines from Taiwan for the department to use.

Individual Rights Defense

I was injured in 2007 while adjusting a machine. In the hospital, I received some legal education resources from an NGO. It was the first time I had heard of such organizations. I chatted with them for some time and thought, "This isn't bad." Later, I began to study the law, like how to calculate wages and how to resign. Originally, I had thought that you needed your superior's approval to resign, and that the wage they offered you was all you could get. Only by studying did I learn that the days worked should be calculated as 21.75 days per month,[12] and other things, such as how to calculate overtime rates.

I began to fight for my individual rights in 2012. The first time I registered a complaint was to report that the dining fee was deducted from our wages (270 yuan per month) whether we ate at the cafeteria or not, that we didn't receive wage slips (*gongzitiao*), that child labor was being employed, and that the factory was not paying into the pension program. I sent a letter to the Labor Bureau listing these problems and asking them to rectify the situation. The inspectors came, but they didn't go to the shop floor—they just walked through the offices. I knew that my letter was the only reason they had come. A few days later, I went to the Bureau to ask about the results. They said there was no problem and that everything was being done legally. I was outraged. I said, "The day that you went, you didn't even leave the air-conditioned rooms. You didn't even talk to any workers." They said they would go again the next week without notifying the boss first, that they would just go straight to the shop floor and do the inspection. When I went back, I told a few managers I was close to that, in a few days, someone would come and inspect the factory. There was a range of opinions among the workers, supervisors, and foremen. Some were supportive, some sat on the sidelines, and there were even some who made sarcastic remarks behind my back. When the labor inspectors came, they telephoned and asked me to meet them in the factory office. I had requested anonymity in my letter of complaint, so I refused to go. I told them to come to the shop floor. They came, but they brought the administrative manager with them. In short, the managers learned that I was the one who had filed the complaint.

It wasn't long before the boss's secretary came looking for me while I was at work. She said I had been causing problems and never asked whether the other employees also wanted pensions. I acted confused and said I didn't know what she was talking about.

The boss began to take his revenge on me. They transferred me to the production line so my wage was several hundred yuan less per month. They also denied me overtime work.

After I was demoted, I called the government service hotline 12345[13] and complained that the labor inspectors had leaked my personal information to the boss. The inspector drove to the factory and said he had not leaked my information. As for how the management found out, he couldn't say. Calling 12345 may be effective for small things, but for big things it's absolutely useless. Later, during the strike, we called every day, and every time they simply said, "There's still no response to the information you submitted. You have to continue waiting."

During the two months I spent working on the production line, I sent a letter of complaint to the local Social Insurance Bureau regarding the factory's lack of Social Insurance. The letter was returned to me unopened in its original envelope. The day I received the returned letter, the district Social Insurance Bureau happened to be holding a conference about problems with health insurance. I participated as a "netizen representative" (*wangmin daibiao*) and personally gave my letter to the bureau's director. I said that our factory was not paying into the pension system. I requested that they make up for the missing payments, and that the management pay late fees. The director said he would personally take up the matter.

Less than two days later, the township Social Insurance Station called me, speaking kindly and apologizing. Later, Boss

Two called me into his office. He said there had been a misunderstanding due to poor communication. He asked me to return to my old position and said I would not be treated poorly. He also told me to stop breaching the chain of command. I returned to my old position. Throughout, I didn't tell my wife about any of this. I only told her I wasn't working overtime. The money I lost because of my demotion that month was never compensated.

The cafeteria arrangement was modified: those who didn't eat there no longer had their pay deducted. Shortly thereafter, they stopped using child labor. They also began distributing wage slips, but the slips had no specific information on them: they had no dates, and not even the word "wage" appeared on them. It was just a number. I went directly to the finance department and said, "There's nothing on it. I can't read this."

When I was fighting for my rights on an individual basis like this, I did consider the consequences. If the boss had told me to resign, I would have refused and then awaited his next move. I thought that at the very least, something positive would come out of it. I kept this up for two months while my supervisors snidely suggested that I resign and give up. Still, I persevered.

As for the Housing Fund,[14] I sent the Social Insurance Bureau a letter about that. They responded that I was correct and they would implement it as soon as possible. Later, the factory made an announcement that they would begin paying into the Housing Fund, but that they would not offer back compensation. We didn't ask for compensation, and some workers didn't want to pay into the Housing Fund. Many simply didn't understand how these programs worked.

One day an administrative manager called out to me in the hallway. He was from the same town I was from. He told me to stop messing around and just do my job. He said even though he was a manager, if it was someone from his hometown who caused problems, people would think he was involved somehow. I replied perfunctorily, "Okay, for the sake of our hometown's reputation, I won't cause any problems." Actually, I had no personal relationship with him.

Our factory had no union. Initially, I wanted to start one, but when I got wind of the 2013 relocation, I knew there was no need to form a union. A union isn't something that can be formed in just a few days. I never told my wife about these rights-defense activities because I didn't want her to worry.

Factory Relocation and Strike

In 2009, our factory began granting any request for resignation. After those who wanted to resigned, there were only four hundred or so employees left.

Shortly before the 2013 Chinese New Year, senior management put out the word that the factory was going to completely relocate to Huizhou. We were skeptical. Then a factory representative announced at an all-staff New Year's banquet that the entire factory would be relocated in six months. Almost all the employees at the banquet began discussing a single question: What will we do if the factory leaves? When two workers met, the most they could say was, "Are you going to Huizhou? I'm not going. . . . If you don't, what will you do?" Circles formed in each department as workers began communicating with one another.

The most active members of these circles were the management personnel and the common workers with more seniority. Most employees had worked there for five or six years, but some had been there for more than ten. The circles were relatively loose; they were just for sharing information. For example, employees from the warehousing department were in contact with the boss more frequently, so they discovered that he had already stopped buying materials. Similarly, the production management department passed along the news that all orders were being sent to Huizhou for completion. Information was thus pieced together among the various circles.

One day, about half a month before the strike, we decided to hold a small meeting to formally discuss the relocation and unify our demands and actions. In addition to myself, there were about a dozen others, all from management. One was an assistant manager and the others were foremen. It was the first time I had discussed these issues with other employees. Afterward, I summarized a bit for the other mechanics, saying some people were sticking their necks out to ask the boss for compensation. My coworkers thought that as long as someone took the lead, they would be willing to follow along.

One assistant manager wasn't willing to show his face at the meeting. He hid in the back and said, "You go ahead and do it, I'm not opposed. If it works, everyone will benefit." He didn't offer any specific opinions; his only contribution was to reveal that the boss had been searching for a furniture factory and was preparing to put down a deposit. Later, however, he served as a witness against us. Instead of testifying in court he provided a verbal testimony at the police station. He said that I had organized the strike but couldn't say whether I had told the workers to block the road.

Hardly any managers were willing to move to Huizhou, not even that administrative manager from my hometown. In the end, only two moved. One was a supervisor who later testified against me, and the other was the warehouse supervisor. Huizhou's factory already had its own team in place, so the managers who went had nothing to do. They had a hard time. Of the managers who didn't go to Huizhou, some returned to their hometowns, some worked elsewhere as clerks, and some took jobs in construction.

Three days before the strike, several of us split up to tell the other workers to meet at a remote location outside the factory for a second meeting. To prevent snitching, we informed only those whom we knew to be reliable. Almost all the forty or fifty people we told came. Most of our discussion was focused on two items. The first was unifying our demands, and the second was deciding when to begin—before or after the machinery was moved. We decided to wait until they put the machinery on the truck to call the strike. If the machines weren't loaded up yet, the boss could say the truck wasn't for moving machinery, that it had been parked there for loading other things. But with the machine on the truck, he would be under pressure on two fronts: from us and from the owner of the truck. The truck was rented, and who knew how much the boss would have to pay each day? Sure enough, once we started negotiating, the boss's first condition was that we release the truck.

During that meeting, everyone said that the base wage in Huizhou was too low. It was only 1,080 yuan per month, so no one was willing to go. We designated liaisons who would be responsible for communicating among the departments and conveying information to the other workers. For example, they would notify everyone that the relocation was indeed imminent, ask whether people wanted to move with the factory, and if not, what should be done. To serve as liaisons, we chose the most active employees. They were not necessarily managers.

The meeting was called because they had moved some machinery that day. We were unprepared, so no one had acted. At the meeting everyone said, "Forget the ones they took today. Next time they try to take a machine, we will act." The specific day was also decided because we had learned from higher-level sources when the next set of machines was to be moved.

After the second meeting, all the shop floor workers knew there would be a strike. They also all knew they would be blocking the truck.

The First Day of the Strike

As soon as we had clocked in that morning, people began sending us updates on the situation outside. "A flatbed truck has arrived!" "Now a crane just pulled up!" "They've loaded one of the machines! "Now they've loaded another one!" "The truck is getting ready to drive off," and so on. At that point, workers from the warehousing department came out and blocked the truck. It was easiest for them because their department was closest to the factory gates.

Once the truck was blocked, all departments switched off the electricity. That way the workers could gather together and no one could say, "I'm not going out. You can go raise a ruckus if you want, but I'll just sit here so the boss won't blame me."

To block the truck, our coworkers from the warehouse dropped forklift pallets in front of it. Then they began taking up spots in the shade because it was so hot outside. At first, the driver kept trying to drive out, but each time he pressed on the gas, workers surrounded the truck to stop it. After a few times, he just turned off the truck and left. By this time, almost all the employees had come out. Only a few supervisors stayed inside. Boss Two's secretary had the supervisors come down and try to persuade us to get back to work, even telling us to go ahead and resign if we refused. Everyone already had a belly full of fire, and hearing that only made it burn hotter.

No one was in charge when the truck was blocked, but once the action had begun, we immediately wrote a "Notice to All Coworkers" and posted it in the factory. Twenty liaisons were chosen, one or two from each department. Then we wrote a list of demands. After some discussion, we decided to collect ten yuan from each worker, in order to start a strike fund.

The security guards were giving us updates about Boss Two: where he went, when he would be back, and so on. They told us they were watching the factory, saying, "As long as the boss knows we're still working, he won't get rid of us. Plus, we can ensure your safety." They even let us drink water from the guard room and use their fans to cool off. But the head of security stayed out of sight and didn't show his face.

Someone from the factory called the police on us. Meanwhile, we called the labor station, which sent someone over who just took our list of demands and left. We said we needed to have the Big Boss come out, since he was the factory's legal representative.

That afternoon we selected eight delegates. Five of them were foremen and three were common workers. We conducted the selection behind a group of buildings so Boss Two's secretary couldn't see what was happening. The whole process took only a few minutes. "These will be the delegates. Do you agree or not? Raise your hand if you agree." The delegates were all relatively well-spoken. They were from different departments, so they didn't all know one another. One woman was chosen as a delegate because she spoke eloquently and was courageous. I didn't know her beforehand; I just knew she worked in quality control. I wasn't really familiar with any of the managers who served as delegates. In the small social circles that had formed, everyone knew which workers in their department were always asking about this kind of thing, so when we had the meeting, we knew who to nominate.

It must have been that afternoon that a cop drove up. He honked his horn and yelled, "Have one worker come out." When we ignored him, he came in. My coworkers asked me to give him our list of demands. Without even glancing at the contents, he crumpled it up on the spot. At that point, I had already turned and was walking away. He pointed at me and said, "You come here!" I didn't listen. The workers gathered around and some female workers began to yell at him. He ran into an office building, snuck out the back and tried to climb over a wall to escape, but he couldn't get over it. Later, another officer came from the police department. He said he was the shift leader and wanted us to step into the office building to chat. I didn't go in because I knew they wouldn't understand the situation, even if I explained it to them. He called me to one side and said that the other officer had had a few drinks at lunch. He also said they were all from my hometown. He wanted me to explain the situation to the other workers. We said, "We want him to apologize, and we want you to guarantee our safety." When the officer came out to apologize, he talked some nonsense about "my Chinese dream." It was already late, so the workers just asked him to leave.

The First Few Days

For the first few days, the labor station and the police department each sent someone by every day. None of the visits lasted more than ten minutes. They would look to see whether we were being good and leave when they saw there was nothing wrong. One time several workers approached them and were told, "You're actually being quite reasonable. That's commendable." This was because, during the first few days of the strike, none of the workers had left the factory. Instead, they just staged sit-ins, so when they saw the inspectors, they would chat with them and even share the water they had bought. When they approached the police and labor station personnel, it was as if they were "speaking bitterness" (*suku*), letting off steam and saying, "We've been waiting for days, the boss ran away and is ignoring us!"

The strike fund we had collected was used to buy water, to pay for delegates' transportation to go petition the government, and to purchase supper for workers who stayed up for the night watch. On the first day of the strike, seven or eight workers went to the District Labor Bureau together with one or two of the liaisons.

Not everything was planned in advance. When the workers thought of something, they would bring it up, such as the idea of organizing a night watch and buying them bread and cookies. We delegates would then discuss the ideas proposed by our coworkers and try to integrate them. Among the eight delegates, one other delegate and I did a large share of the talking, while some delegates said nothing. It wasn't just the delegates who participated in the meetings; the liaisons also took part, so there were often twenty or thirty people at the meetings. Sometimes we also substituted for the liaisons, because the original liaison had to take care of something and we needed someone to communicate with the other workers.

We told outsiders the delegates weren't chosen until the Big Boss came, which was several days after the strike began, but they were actually selected on the first day. If something came up, all eight delegates discussed it. There were meetings every morning and evening. One or two delegates would gather twenty or thirty other workers to keep watch through the night, lest the boss sneak in and make off with the truck. All our meetings were held in the onsite dormitories. Our initial work went rather well. No matter what the boss did, he was unable to rattle us. If something came up, it was discussed at the meetings and arrangements were made. But beneath the surface, things were bad. The workers were not united, nor were the workers' delegates. The boss divided us and broke us. That assistant manager was separated from us. He said the boss had a background in organized crime and would use his gangster connections to deal with us. As time went on, the workers became impatient and impulsive. Sometimes we had trouble locating people, and it was hard to make decisions.

Nearby, there was another factory that relocated. The boss paid the workers' delegates twenty thousand yuan each to make off during the second day of negotiations, and there was no one to negotiate. We discussed that incident.

At the time, I estimated the strike would be resolved within seven days because there was a great deal of products waiting to be shipped. One day after the strike began, there was an overseas client who called me asking to release the products. He said he wanted to take the cabinets. That man spoke Mandarin so well that I couldn't tell he was a foreigner. When we went to the offices of the All-China Federation of Trade Unions (ACFTU) or the Labor Bureau, we always left my phone number. It wasn't something we thought about beforehand, because we didn't know those places required a number to leave a complaint.

From the time the strike was called until the first day of negotiations, the delegates remained optimistic. We met daily and assigned tasks. For example, we sent a few people to deliver some documents to the municipal ACFTU office. When they came back, there was another meeting to discuss the ACFTU's attitude. When people came from the police department or the Labor Bureau, we asked someone to meet them. Afterward we held meetings to disseminate their comments to our fellow workers.

The municipal office of the ACFTU expressed no position. They simply said, "We accept these documents from you." The district office called us and said that the ACFTU is led by the Chinese Communist Party (CCP) and cannot separate itself from the party, so we would have to contact the local party committee to resolve the matter. If there were results, we could then report them to the ACFTU office. Beyond that, we had no further contact with the ACFTU.

After the workers went out onto the street and blocked traffic, the assistant secretary of the Subdistrict CCP Work Committee began meeting with us every day. We thought that notifying the Subdistrict Petitions Office was the same as notifying the CCP, because in general, if you are trying to contact the party, they say, "Go to the Petitions Office."

One day, we saw some unidentifiable people at the factory gates. None of the workers' delegates believed the boss would send people to attack us, but we were thinking about how we would get away once we had been compensated. We thought we would get a vehicle ready and, when we were compensated, the delegates would be compensated first. Then the delegates would ensure that everyone was paid and that those who had been paid did not leave. Finally, everyone would leave together. The workers' delegates would get directly into their vehicle and find a place to hide out for a few days.

One day after the strike began, I heard through the grapevine that Boss Two said he would rather spend ten million yuan fighting the workers than give them a single penny. Somebody said that Boss Two told certain people this in confidence; it was not said at the negotiating table. The managers gave us this information to dissuade us from carrying on. We did a rough calculation that if everyone were compensated according to the law, it would not exceed four or five million yuan. It would certainly be less than ten million.

Before the strike, I saw news of a nearby strike on the television. When the strike broke out in our factory, I went directly to that factory to examine the situation. They were also dealing with a factory relocation, and it was bad. The boss had already moved all the machines and resumed production in the new location. The factory grounds were rented and the water and electricity had been cut off. Only a few dozen workers were still trying to put up a fight. I discussed it with them. They were refusing to accept the boss's offer of 30 percent of the amount they demanded and insisted on 100 percent. As a result, they had to follow the recommendations of the district government and begin labor arbitration, which was going to take forty to fifty days. Waiting so long made them furious and a bit nervous. If the arbitration results were bad, they could lose even that 30 percent!

I told the workers' delegates and liaisons about it. If that was the process for labor arbitration, we certainly could not apply. So, whenever the judge recommended arbitration, the workers' delegates unanimously opposed it. I said arbitration would take forty to fifty days at best, six months at worst. Furthermore, the risk was high. None of us wanted arbitration; we wanted to speak face-to-face with the boss.

The Third Day of the Strike

The Big Boss drove up with the head of security and told us that he would not relocate the factory. He asked us to return to work without compensation. There were several hundred people listening there to him, and everyone yelled, "If you say you're not moving, don't move! The machines are already on the truck." He had no interest in discussing it and left. The workers didn't think of stopping him then. The Big Boss often came down to the shop floor and chatted with workers. At Mid-Autumn Festival, he would distribute two moon cakes, one piece of fruit, and one beverage. He was usually quite kind to the managers and employees, so some workers believed him. They said, "The Big Boss said the factory isn't relocating. If he says so, it's true." A small group of employees planned to return to work the next day. The workers' delegates didn't show up the next morning. Instead, we decided to have several female employees defend the punch clocks so no one could clock in. As soon as we announced this, those employees gave up on going because it would have been boring anyway. The workers' delegates didn't plan to forcibly obstruct the workers, just to verbally persuade them not to work.

The Sixth Day of the Strike

A small truck came from Huizhou to take the molds. We blocked the truck from leaving. The boss had rented the truck from an individual in Huizhou. Everyone agreed we were not going to let him take even a single screw through the factory gates. The driver didn't know the situation in the factory, but he said he'd been sent by the boss to take the molds to Huizhou. My coworkers said our factory was on strike. The driver didn't know what to say, asking, "How is that possible? I'm doing business. The boss told me to come so I came." The workers refused to release his car, so he just left without it. In the beginning, we actually had quite a few bargaining chips. But when the boss promised he would pay, we let all the vehicles go. We made a good faith effort at negotiating. How could we know the boss was leading us on?

That afternoon, the director of the subsidiary factory came to us with a lawyer. That day it was my turn to take a break, so I was not at the factory. The workers called me, saying the director's car was there and they planned to prevent it from leaving. They went to the guard room and found that the car had not been registered, so they blocked the gates. The director was furious. He said it was his private car, but the workers said it belonged to the factory. In response, the director called the police. A van full of riot police arrived, but they didn't enter the factory. Seeing that the Special Police had arrived, the workers surrounded the factory gate to stop the director's car from leaving.[15] They wanted to see what would happen and whether people would be seized. The workers made preparations.

I hurried to the factory gates on my electric bike, but they stopped me from entering. The police chief told me to release the factory director's car or they would seize me and take me to the station. I said, "What does it have to do with me? If you want the car, have the workers release it. If you want to seize them, seize them." I paid him no heed and just ran to the workers to ask what was going on. They told me the lawyer had come. I asked him what the situation was, and he said he had come to speak to the workers' delegates. I said that was fine, and we arranged a time the next day to meet in the factory's conference room.

After the lawyer left, we held a meeting to discuss what we would say the next day. We decided eight people would go together, but that one other delegate and I would do most of the talking. We also invited a labor rights lawyer.

The Seventh Day of the Strike

From ten to eleven o'clock in the morning, we negotiated at the factory. The boss's lawyer came to the discussion, as did someone from the Labor Bureau and the lawyer we had asked to come. The boss's lawyer told us the factory was not relocating. We countered with five demands: economic compensation, high-temperature subsidies, payment into the pension system, compensation for the failure to provide paid vacation time, and triple wages for working on national holidays. The management's lawyer said he had no authority to act. That was it—the morning negotiation yielded no results. Still, we thought that was probably normal in such negotiations and prepared for the next round.

At noon, the management suddenly called and informed us we would continue negotiations at two o'clock. We called our lawyer to come back.

At two, we returned to the conference room and found that the room had been outfitted with cameras that had not been there in the morning. This time Boss Two came. He took out a statement and read it. It said that the factory was not relocating and that the workers must return to work. Those who did not would be fired if their absence continued for three more days. Furthermore, he wanted the workers to pay compensation for the losses that the factory had accrued during the strike. When he had finished, the man from the Labor Bureau said they had found no violations of the law when they inspected the factory. He said that because the factory was not currently relocating, we should get back to work, or else we would just be pointlessly causing trouble. Then they stopped speaking to us.

Outraged, I yelled, "Is it or is it not illegal for the management to refuse to pay into our pension programs? Is it or is it not illegal for the management to. . . . " First, he was relocating the factory. The machinery was already loaded onto the truck that we had blocked in, so he had no grounds to deny that. Second, they had never paid into our pensions. They also provided no annual leave, no statutory holiday pay, and no high-temperature subsidies. How could they say that the factory was not violating the law? Then there were the problems with the wage slips, which weren't done according to the Shenzhen municipal regulations for payments. It was completely impossible to make sense of anything on the slips—they were just sheets of paper with nothing but a few numbers on them, not even the month. I told them all of this, saying, "Are you just speaking nonsense with your eyes wide open? There are so many violations in this factory, and you still say the management hasn't broken any laws."

Basically, the management's attitude was that they weren't having a discussion. Our lawyer saw the situation and left without saying anything or speaking to the workers' delegates about what to do next. He knew that if he stayed and things got out of control, he might be blamed for it.

After the lawyer left, we went out and reported the results of the negotiations to the workers. When the workers heard how awful the situation was, they flew into a burning rage. Everyone rushed out and blocked the North Ring Road, but the riot police arrived immediately—they had obviously prepared for this. Within half an hour, they had forced the workers back to the factory. One female worker's arm was broken.

When the workers arrived back at the factory, the work-day was still not over. There were still administrators, including Boss Two, in the office building, so we surrounded it. Soon a government representative went in as well. While we were staging a sit-in outside the building, one worker collapsed from a heart attack. It was a matter of life and death, but the management still took no action. I don't know what they were thinking. From a humanitarian viewpoint, something should have been done. It was situations like this that allowed the workers to see through the management, making them even angrier.

When we surrounded the building, the labor station director intervened and tried to persuade us to step down. The workers demanded that Boss Two come out and explain why he had reversed his statement. We waited for an hour or two, but he stayed hidden in his office. Instead of breaking in, we insisted that he step outside. The police didn't enter the factory yard, but management sent people to patrol the premises on motorcycles—all of them people hired just for this purpose. When Boss Two finally came out, he just said stuff like, "I'm not authorized to make decisions," and "I can't act as a legal representative."

We heard rumors that the factory owners would "use criminal gangs to deal with the workers' delegates." Just in case, I released this information on my microblog.

After that, five of the workers' delegates stepped down, including both managers and common workers, so we selected five new delegates from the liaisons. Eventually, we talked the original five delegates into coming back and had those replacements go back to serving as liaisons.

The Eighth Day of the Strike

My coworkers went first thing in the morning to the subdistrict government office. Boss Two came with his entourage, because the subdistrict office had requested his presence. There were roughly three hundred workers who went. They sat in groups of two or three on the lawn outside the office and held a banner that had been hastily written in ink. The decision to petition with a sit-in was spontaneous. It was not a decision taken by the workers' delegates, none of whom took part. The boss had refused to negotiate the day before, and if it were impossible to negotiate, then there was no reason for the workers' delegates to be present. The subdistrict office seems not to have known that workers were going to petition, otherwise it would have stopped them in advance. I was at my place when the subdistrict office called and asked me to go to the scene. Upon arriving, I saw that a mass of police officers had moved to surround the workers on two sides. Even with the group surrounded, they still could not locate the workers' delegates because none of us had gone—that's why they had phoned me. Shortly thereafter, the government said that the boss had agreed to negotiate, so we delegates should convince our coworkers to go home. The Big Boss spoke to us through the government. That time, the subdistrict office didn't detain anyone and even promised to help us resolve the issue.

Conveying all of this to the workers went smoothly. We said the boss had promised to compensate us and that he had agreed to meet at the labor station conference room at three o'clock the next afternoon. The second round of negotiations would be focused on specific issues.

The delegates thought things were developing in a positive direction, but we also discussed the need to force the boss back to the bargaining table if discussions broke down. I felt we had to negotiate from an equal position. I even said to the management, "The negotiations must be done in good faith. You can't be overbearing. Don't think that just because we're your employees, we're like a lower caste in some ancient feudal society, or like indentured laborers before the revolution, and that therefore we have to obey you. That's not a negotiation, right?" The workers saw right through their conspiratorial methods. Actually, every day there were also workers who said that we delegates weren't bold enough and called for us to take to the streets.

The Ninth Day of the Strike

The next morning, I was invited to chat with the police's political instructor (*jiaodaoyuan*). He pressured me not to post on my microblog and spoke to me of morality, even bringing in Mao Zedong: "I listen to Mao's words. . . . One word from him is like ten thousand words from another"—that kind of weird junk. Essentially, he wanted me to stop pressuring the government by posting on my microblog. In addition, he told me to have low expectations for that afternoon's negotiation, and to convey that to the other workers. What he said to me seemed half in jest. It certainly didn't seem particularly serious.

Laughing, I said, "Sure, as long as the government comes out and organizes the negotiations, it's no different to me whether I'm posting on social media or not. If you facilitate the negotiations, what good would it do us to post anything?" I also said, "The blog isn't illegal, by the way. If the negotiations don't produce any results, I'm definitely going to post about it. The blog's not for riling up workers but to record what the workers are up to every day and what happens. I'm not fabricating anything." In any case, I said that my posts were not illegal, and that if I needed to post something, I would do so. He didn't say that I would be detained if I posted again. He just laughed and said it didn't matter because the government was going to show up. He told me to trust the government and the party.

They also knew about the NGO. They said such organizations were agents of foreign powers with ulterior motives and urged me not to get involved with them. I said we didn't know what to do and had no choice but to seek out such organizations for ideas. At this point, a uniformed police officer sitting nearby spoke up, saying he wanted to learn more about this NGO, that I should introduce him some time. He mentioned that we both came from the same part of China. My first impression was that he was a good person because he expressed empathy for us.

Not long after I left the police station, I got a call from my landlord saying he would no longer rent to me and that

I had five days to move out. I immediately called the police station and said, "How could you do this? What you're doing is unconscionable!" They just said, "We'll help you resolve this problem." I went to see the landlord. Just when I found him, the police officer gave me a call and I handed the phone to the landlord. Ultimately, he agreed to let me stay.

I think they had discussed things with the bosses early on and agreed on their bargaining chips in advance. At that point, the police asked me to come in to the station alone. I thought they wouldn't possibly detain me, but still I told the other workers' delegates about it, and two or three of them went to the entrance of the station to wait for me. Later, the bosses sought out my relatives and hometown friends to put pressure on me. When the factory had started relocating in 2006, some of my relatives and friends had transferred to the Huizhou site. Now the bosses had them call and tell me to stop causing problems and just do my job in peace. They even asked me to move to Huizhou, though they didn't say how I might benefit from that—they couldn't promise anything. They probably weren't really pressured to call me. I just joked, "Okay, okay, I'll move right over. You rent me an apartment." Because they were my relatives, they just laughed.

That afternoon, the second round of negotiations was held at the Labor Bureau. The police told us to be prepared, but who could have known what a shockingly terrible offer the boss would make? Just three hundred yuan! We were baffled. They told us not to expect too much, but who knew it would be so little?

When the negotiation started, the Big Boss arrived. He was acting pathetic and said he had a cold. He asked us to look at the needle tracks on his arms.[16] He told us he had never been cruel to the workers and talked about how all those years he had worked himself to death finding orders for the factory. He said that at least he gave the workers opportunities to work overtime so they could earn a little extra money. The clothes he wore were very ordinary. Boss Two was the same way. Though he kept his wardrobe cleaner and tidier, the clothing was not expensive. Boss Two's secretary, however, dressed extremely well, as if she were a model. She made extra money for herself by taking scraps from the factory every Saturday in her truck and selling them. This had been going on for a couple years already. Those materials were expensive—she could make as much as ten thousand yuan for one truckload.

After the Big Boss showed his face, he left. He simply replied that he would compensate us (without specifying how much) and asked us to discuss the specifics with the lawyers and the administrative manager. We all thought we would be able to reach an agreement with him. There were one or two hundred workers waiting outside the labor station.

When we began discussing it with the lawyer, he said they would give us three hundred yuan [of compensation, per year worked]. Even though we had prepared, that still shocked us. A handout for a beggar! We refused.

Before the negotiations, my expectation was two thousand yuan [of compensation, per year worked]. We thought that the other side would use the lowest wage as a bottom limit, so we just added up the numbers and got two thousand yuan. Considering that overtime and statutory holiday pay were included, this was not unreasonable. Both parties could discuss the price and make counteroffers, but how would we know they would offer three hundred yuan? Before the negotiations, I said we shouldn't split the workers into groups based on their wages because if we did, those with lower wages would stop fighting. I also worked to persuade the managers, saying it was a per person cost. Once the strike was called, we would discuss a single demand of two thousand yuan [of compensation, per year worked] for both managers and common workers. The managers who took part were largely drawn from the lower-level management, and all of them wholeheartedly agreed.

I was supposed to be the lead negotiator, but the other delegates began chaotically speaking out of turn and saying three hundred would not work. When the lawyer said three hundred yuan, we asked for two thousand. The lawyer said two thousand was pretty high, so he would have to ask the Big Boss. He called the boss on the spot and said the Big Boss had agreed to four hundred yuan [of compensation per year worked]. We said we would not accept that and wanted to continue negotiating. Ultimately, the lawyer said the Hong Kong board of directors had looked into the matter and decided to add another hundred, bringing the offer to five hundred. We said, "No way, that's still far too low."

By the time we got to five hundred yuan, the sky had already grown dark. We said we were done talking for the day and agreed to meet again two days later. At the end, the lawyer told us the Big Boss felt there was no point in us continuing to hold the truck, considering that negotiations were already underway. He said the boss had been forthcoming, so it was our turn to show that we were negotiating in good faith. This turned out to be a trap. We had initially assumed that he would be unwilling to negotiate, but now he was, so we said, "All right, all right, we'll show that we're in good faith." Several of us discussed it a bit and agreed that we would release the truck but the machinery could not be moved. It would be unloaded and stored inside the factory.

The delegates held a short, hushed conversation on the matter and reached an agreement. There were those who opposed it, but they were in the minority. We also considered the fact that so long as the truck was at the factory, we had to assign people to guard it every day. It was a big hassle to watch it at night. There were mosquitoes, and everyone hated doing it. At first people had actively volunteered for the night watch, but by this point, we had to assign the task by rotating among the departments. If the truck were released, the workers would be a bit more relaxed. So we decided to just let it go.

We assumed that after one more discussion it would be over and we would be able to get at least sixteen hundred yuan. We promised the other workers we would not go lower than sixteen hundred yuan. I still had hope, because from three hundred, to four hundred, to five hundred yuan, the offer was increasing.

The director of the labor station had chaired the negotiations. The opposing side was made up of four or five people, and everyone from the police station was downstairs. A man from the Labor Bureau recorded the meeting, but we didn't record it. We didn't realize we would need a record.

At seven o'clock that evening, the administrative manager phoned us again to confirm because he was worried some workers would raise a fuss when the truck was released, but everything went smoothly. There were only a few hundred workers there.

It was impossible to notify every single worker about the decision to release the truck: some were out on their bikes, while others were doing part-time handicraft jobs at home. This just goes to show how little solidarity there was among the workers. Those who weren't at the factory had no idea what was happening. The majority of those at the factory agreed, so we released the truck.

Throughout everything, the government seemed to be standing on our side. They said to our faces, "We're going to get rid of that boss of yours. If he doesn't leave, we won't let him operate here." The director of the Labor Bureau said those words. The lawyers and the Labor Bureau personnel never said we were acting illegally by holding the truck. Once, when someone from the Labor Bureau came to the factory and saw we were blocking the truck, they even said we should stop the boss from taking a single screw. That made us feel better. We thought they were speaking for us and assumed the government was putting pressure on the boss, but our appraisal of the situation was overly optimistic.

The Tenth Day of the Strike

The boss locked the doors to the offices and the factory building. We held a meeting about what we would do the next day and how we would hold out for sixteen hundred yuan.

The Eleventh Day of the Strike

The third round of negotiations was at three o'clock that afternoon, but this time was different. The bosses did not appear. Only the lawyer, the administrative manager, and a clerk took part. The negotiations were held at the Labor Bureau, and, as soon as we met, we discovered their attitude was completely different. The lawyer told us the bosses had decided the most they could pay was five hundred yuan. That was to say, there was nothing to discuss. They just said the amount would be five hundred and it made no difference whether we discussed it or not. After all the struggles we had been through over the past ten days, this was the only result. We informed the workers immediately. They were furious and began to raise a ruckus around the labor station.

The lawyer said he was unable to make any decisions, so we demanded that he call the boss. The boss said he didn't care, and the lawyer responded, "You may not care, but I'm here surrounded by workers." The boss said, "Let them go ahead and surround you. You just sit there." The lawyer said he would never take a case like this again. Meanwhile, the director of the labor station said nothing. Some workers began to complain. They said they had never agreed to release the truck, and now the boss had changed his tune. At that point, the workers' delegates seemed to be of two minds.

Later on, a portion of the workers went to the subdistrict government office to protest and blocked the road in front of it. That was right when people got off work, and this time the subdistrict took action. The one or two hundred workers who were blocking the road were detained and taken to the police station. Fights broke out, and two or three female workers were wounded. They spent the night in the hospital receiving intravenous drips.

The workers' delegates didn't go with them to the subdistrict office, but the liaisons did. In some situations, the workers' delegates had to avoid suspicion. None of the workers' delegates participated in any of the militant actions taken by other workers.

After our coworkers were taken to the police station, the

chief of police called and asked me to come talk to the workers (*zuo sixiang gongzuo*). When I arrived, I found they were being held in the station's athletic field. There were Community Defense officers (*lianfangduiyuan*) and Special Police there—in total between one and two hundred officers. I would guess the Community Defense officers came from several different neighborhoods. They were all standing close to the workers, but they were unarmed. Inside the main room of the station, there were also many regular police in uniform.

When the station bought the Community Defense officers boxed meals, the workers yelled that they had not been fed and were hungry. They stole some of the food and ate it.

This continued until eleven o'clock at night, when the chief of police decided to send the workers home, but they refused to go. They had been taken to the station in buses, and they wanted the buses to take them back. The police chief urged us to convince the workers to go home because it had begun to rain. They gave me a loudspeaker and I said to them, "It's raining. Let's just go home and forget about it."

The Twelfth and Thirteenth Days of the Strike

Saturday and Sunday were quiet and without incident. A few dozen of us, including the workers' delegates and liaisons, discussed our next steps. Some people recommended going together to the factory's office building, where we would drink water and enjoy the air conditioning until we forced the boss to come back. Until then, we had not entered the building. We were consciously avoiding it, lest the boss accuse us of making trouble.

The Fourteenth Day of the Strike

More than one hundred workers entered the office building. A few clerks were inside working. We didn't disrupt them. Instead, we looked for water and cool spots in the building. Some workers just sat in the meeting rooms with the air conditioning turned on. None of the workers was very young, and there were no hotheads, so there was no vandalism. Everyone just went in to enjoy the air conditioning. The boss's things were not tampered with.

That day, the subdistrict government's Secretary for Political and Legal Affairs visited. Upon arrival, he contacted the factory director and asked him to come. It was already after eight o'clock at that point. The factory director brought along a lawyer and a foreigner who was a customer of the factory. A batch of products had been sitting in the warehouse, and they said the shipping deadline had arrived so they needed to move them right away. But the workers had developed bellies full of fire ever since the truck had been released, and they were dead set against releasing the products.

Just when we were about to discuss it, the man from the government left. The factory director wanted to leave with him, but the workers wouldn't let him go. They kept him in the office building until two o'clock in the morning. Finally, he wrote a promise that he would come back for another discussion at nine o'clock, as did the director of the labor station, signing his name. We believed them and prepared to resume negotiations.

The Fifteenth Day of the Strike

That morning, someone from the Labor Bureau asked me to come out so they could record a testimony. From the first day of the strike until then, it was the first time they had collected documents of any kind. I think the Labor Bureau just wanted to avoid responsibility and ensure that they could claim they had not been negligent, that they had been actively investigating the matter and taking statements. I was already thinking of all of this when I went in. They didn't really want to resolve the problems—this was just to formally put the matter on file. On the first day of the strike, we had gone to them for help, but instead of starting a file, they just delayed. Now that they saw how our boss was acting, they had no choice but to have us make statements. There were several delegates who knew I was headed to the labor station, but the others were unaware.

When I went, we had come up with a new demand: for them to help resolve our problems obtaining food and water.

They had all kinds of food in the factory, along with cooks and kitchen equipment. But once the struggle had begun, the cafeteria stopped operating. We requested that the government come forward and reopen the cafeteria so the workers could have something to eat and calm down, rather than going out on the streets demonstrating. The subdistrict's Secretary for Political and Legal Affairs made a written promise to send a task force to the factory to discuss feeding the workers and what would happen if the boss ran off.

When I returned to the factory from the labor station, I found that two or three hundred workers had already gone out onto the streets. I thought it was strange that they were carrying a banner—turns out they had it printed themselves. This time no one was detained. The workers marched to the subdistrict office and the police walked with them. They even used their motorbikes to control traffic for them.

Something strange happened that night. Despite heavy rain during the day, a small building in the factory complex caught fire and burned to the ground. Inside were waste materials and some mechanical equipment. The guards were at the factory when it caught fire, and I only heard of it the day after. Some workers called me and told me not to come, saying it was already completely destroyed. There were several fire trucks parked outside when I went to the factory to investigate.

The workers began to argue about the fire. Some said the boss had hired someone to start it.

The police detained all the guards who were on duty at the time. We weren't able to contact them and didn't know what was going on. Everyone was terribly nervous. We asked all over trying to figure out how it had happened.

The Sixteenth Day of the Strike

The government sent a task force to the factory to discuss the matter of providing food. Because all the offices were locked, we discussed it in an empty room in the dormitory. The task force included members of the Labor Bureau, the subdistrict government, the Petitions Office, and the Office for Comprehensive Management of Public Security (*zongzhiban*). They came in more than a dozen cars.

Throughout the day, despite multiple rounds of discussion, the issue of supplying food and water was not resolved. There was an official who said he could not agree to the workers' demand that the government provide food. He asked, "How could we feed workers who aren't working for the subdistrict government?" The task force recommended we borrow money from the village committee's corporation, which was the lessor of the factory. We refused because borrowing money would obviously divide the workers and make it impossible to continue the struggle. We said we didn't want their money, we just wanted them to open the cafeteria. As long as there was food and water, that would be enough. But they never gave us a clear answer. The discussions yielded no results and the workers stayed outside shouting.

At seven o'clock in the evening, the task force drove off, leaving the workers there to stew. They began to get rambunctious and said they wanted to go downtown.

At that point, everyone was worn out. Some workers were also scared because of the fire. They didn't know whether the blame would fall on them.

The guards had never stopped working because the boss would have just hired new guards if they had gone on strike. That also would have been bad for the other workers, so the guards continued to take shifts.

Under those circumstances, I could not clearly judge the cause of the fire. I didn't know if the workers had become so enraged that they started it or if the boss had hired someone to do so. In my inability to make an accurate assessment of the matter, I grew panicked and scatterbrained. I didn't know what would happen. So that day I went home early and didn't attend that evening's meeting. The guards had not yet come back, and

I didn't know if the police had reached a conclusion regarding the fire.

There was a journalist who came to investigate the cause of the fire. The government public relations officer obstructed the journalist, following everywhere he went.

A bit later, the guards were released. After investigating for half a day and reviewing the security footage, the police determined that the fire had started naturally and had no connection to the workers.

The Seventeenth Day of the Strike

I was worried there would be trouble, so I came and circled the factory at six o'clock that morning. Everyone had heard about the guards being released. The workers had heard that the fire had no connection to them and felt relieved, so they arrived early at the factory and started raising a ruckus. By eight o'clock there were already a lot of people gathered at the factory gates, some yelling about going to the municipal government. The workers' delegates had yet to arrive.

At roughly nine o'clock, some people from the labor station drove up, but they didn't enter the factory. Instead, they parked their car more than 100 meters away. I went over to speak to them.

Most of the workers did not live on the factory ground, but by this time, the majority of them had already arrived. Everyone was at the factory gates shouting. I saw that someone, I don't know who, had taken out the banner from two days before. They wanted to take to the streets.

Until then, the delegates had been in control during each worker action. During this action, however, we lost control. Some delegates didn't even show up that day.

Seeing everyone surge out of the factory gates, I asked the people from the Labor Bureau to stop the workers from marching, but they refused. We delegates could do nothing to stop the workers at that point. The government refused to act, so they can't put all the blame on us. They just stood there like they were watching a show. Afterward, the director of the labor station repeatedly denied that I had urged them to come out and stop the workers.

It was impossible to dissuade the workers, but I couldn't relax so I followed behind and went with them. While we were walking, the police and some employees of the subdistrict government walked with us.

When we started out, the road was bustling. Lots of people saw us and took photos. Once we had walked for two hours, we came to a place that was far from anyone else. There was a barrier in the road so the cars in the opposing lanes couldn't see what was happening. That's when they seized us. They really chose the perfect spot to take action.

The officers who took us in weren't Community Defense officers. The Community Defense officers had said to us, "We won't seize you. If we hear that we're supposed to seize you, we'll run off. We're workers, too. We want the workers to speak out, because that's the only way we'll get a raise." Their basic monthly wage was only seventeen hundred yuan. Even if you factored in bonuses, et cetera, it was still little more than two thousand yuan, so they were also quite unhappy.

Previously, when the subdistrict office detained us, they sent in the *jixundui* [private policing force]. This time, after we had been detained on the way to the municipal government, it was also the *jixundui* that escorted us. One young member even spoke with us. He said he saw me the other day at the police station imploring the workers to behave themselves, so he couldn't understand why I would march with the workers today. I asked if he was part of the Public Security Bureau, and he said no, that he was "hired" (*zhaopinde*), and that every day they practiced drills for "maintaining stability" (*weiwen*).

The previous time we were seized, it was nighttime and we were far from the main road. No one had taken any extreme actions. Groups of two or three officers had simply grabbed people and loaded them onto the vehicles. But this time it was different. They rushed toward us, grabbing our hair and pressing us to the ground.

They came running right toward me. A group of my coworkers surrounded me to try and stop the seizure, but all the *jixundui* were tall, brawny men, and the workers couldn't hold the line.

I saw workers beaten until blood ran from their mouths. Some had their hair torn out. Everyone was on the ground screaming. It was hard to take. I pushed to the front to try to reason with them. I said we simply wanted our wages and that we weren't bad people. I told them we just wanted the money we had earned through our own sweat and blood. I said, "You have parents, too! You have sisters and parents who are working somewhere."

When we were beaten, we felt fury, not terror.

I was singing the song "Socialism is Good" and crying out, "Long live the Communist Party!"

At first, they didn't know where I was but as soon as I began to shout, they knew. One officer came and identified me. They rushed forward, so I gave up resisting and went with them. For the rest of my life, I'll never forget that scene.

In the end, they drove several tour buses over and took all of the workers. We were sent to separate police stations with twenty or thirty people to a station.

They put handcuffs on me, and I was held in a small room when we arrived at the station. After a few hours in there, an officer came to interrogate me. He said he was from the same part of China as me, and that therefore he had no interest in hurting me. He said it would be no problem for me to make a confession. Once I had read it, I signed. A while later, I decided it was no good and asked to give a new confession. The second time I signed without reading it closely because I was too exhausted. Only during the trial did I discover there were some errors. In the confession, it said that the workers hit the police, and at the end it said things like the workers didn't listen to instructions.

The police said there was no way they would release me that night, and that if they were going to release me, it would be the next morning. The next day everyone except six or seven of us was released. I shouted and protested. I was locked in a room with no air conditioning, and it was sweltering. They had me locked up with several other workers. That evening the *jix-undui* came again. We were separated and given different vests: some were for criminal detention, others for administrative detention. Our vests were red.

In court, I said that I had given multiple confessions but that I didn't closely examine the second one. There was only one person taking my confession, and he didn't inform me of my rights and responsibilities. According to the law, there should be two people asking questions. My lawyer argued that they hadn't complied with procedures. I also told the judge I was handcuffed and taken to a small room after being seized. I was close to having a nervous breakdown, but they questioned me anyway.

The Detention Center

Those of us who remained in custody were identified as key participants. Some had walked in the front of the crowd, some had carried banners, and some had resisted. Aside from myself, two other workers were held for an extended period, thirty-seven days each. One was a workers' delegate and the other was a female worker who apparently hit a police officer. They said they had it on video.

The police station said they would hold me for three days at the most, but I later learned that it could be extended with a notice of extended detention (*yanchang jiya tongzhishu*). We never imagined we would be sentenced.

It wasn't until my release that I learned the workers had tried to pay a bribe. My wife gathered three thousand yuan but was told that would not be enough, so she gathered another two thousand. Still the police refused to release me and returned the money. I didn't see my wife from the time I was detained until the trial.

An advocacy lawyer introduced me to a lawyer. She came to the police station, took one look at me and accepted my three thousand yuan.

Later, I was moved to the district-level detention center. I was held in one unit for ten days and then moved to a different unit where I stayed for the duration. When we went in, the old were separated from the young. There was a processing unit.

It took six months for me to be formally arraigned (*tishen*). I did not admit to marching. I said it was not a march, that it was a spontaneous decision to go petition the government for help. Another person questioned me about the last day. They asked questions like was I the one organizing things on the last day, who made the banner, had I collected the money, and who were the workers' delegates? I said, "You were all wearing helmets and carrying batons. It was just you hitting us. How could we hit you?"

Eating in there, the winter melons weren't peeled, nor were the pumpkins. You had to pay if you wanted to eat a little better. Cigarettes were impossible to buy. The custodial officer could give you cigarettes, but everyone else just smoked the cigarette butts. A third of the people inside were drug traffickers.

The cells were 12 meters long, 3.6 meters wide and could fit 51 persons. The bunks were 2 meters wide and the aisles 1.6 meters. I had a personal blanket. Some others slept on the ground on sheets of paper. Those sleeping on the bottom had to sleep curled up like a dog—they couldn't extend their legs.

We could write letters. Each letter sent to us was opened and read. In the beginning, I was able to receive letters, but later, when the custodial officer (*guanjiao*) found out, I stopped receiving them at all.

In the beginning, I slept on the bottom. Later, I became an "old timer" because I got along with the others pretty well. I explained my situation to them, and they came to believe I wasn't a bad person and that I was innocent. After I was seized, they told me that I would be held for six months at most. If you're held for less than six months, you don't get a criminal record.

Over time, I became impatient. I would punch the bed when I felt upset. Usually, I went running in the mornings and read in the evenings. Sometimes we discussed issues like family, society, and politics just to pass the time. At night, we watched TV. The news came on at seven o'clock. There was one TV in the unit, installed on the wall. It was a bulky Taiwanese model. There were also books to buy. They gave you a book list, and if you chose something, they would send it to you and deduct the cost from your card.

I bought a lot of books. Some were by Lang Xianping and Yu Jianrong [two famous, contemporary, liberal intellectuals] and some were on economics. Outsiders could not send books in. There were a few other prisoners that read books, but you had to choose from the list they gave you.

Some Thoughts on Labor Leaders and Workers' Delegates

In order to carry out labor negotiations, we have to cultivate workers' delegates, not labor leaders. Workers' delegates should be mindful of self-preservation. They cannot be cultivated in just a few days. It takes a long time, and they have to fight alongside the workers. Only when they have formed strong relationships can they truly represent the workers. Workers who serve as delegates for only one or two days of the strike are easily bought off by the owners.

In Guangdong now, there are people in every industrial district and every factory studying labor law and helping their fellow workers to develop consciousness. These are effective methods, and once they become widespread, active elements among the workers will gather and gradually teach people how to negotiate. This safeguards against mishaps. When it comes to specific actions, they will be able to stand up and take on those burdens.

Workers' delegates are, first and foremost, workers. Workers' delegates can serve as a means of communication or a bridge. But workers' delegates are not the same as labor leaders. Leaders have absolute authority. They are willing to step forward with a defiant attitude. The owners and the government do not worry about workers' delegates; they worry about labor leaders.

Labor leaders agitate and build connections between different factories. That's something they're able to do. They stand apart from the workers. In China's current situation, labor leaders have a 100 percent chance of being persecuted. But workers' delegates are different from labor leaders. The delegate is also a worker, and he or she is capable only of serving as a communication channel for the owners and the government.

Labor leaders and workers are distinguished by the fact that the leaders hold absolute authority. What they say goes, and there are no negotiations between them and the workers. A labor leader could be biased or make decisions arbitrarily. Labor leaders are prone to believe that everything is for your own good, and this can create a rift between them and the workers. For now, we remain unable to cultivate labor leaders, and must rely on workers' delegates. I believe that in this moment, the type of labor leader who can democratically represent the workers does not exist.

There is also the issue of uniting the workers and uniting the workers' delegates. There was a point when a supervisor called a worker and asked him to go to the shop floor. The other workers thought he had been bought out, and many people were upset with him. He went to the shop floor but couldn't find the supervisor. When I heard of this, I immediately explained to this coworker why that was wrong. I told everyone they should handle things differently next time. The next time something came up, they were not to take action independently.

There is a slight difference between low-level managers who act as delegates and workers who do. Low-level managers are usually managing workers, so they have to maintain a higher status than the workers. When it comes to taking action, they use administrative methods. But common workers are different. They rely on their own skills. When problems come up, the workers think, "You're not from our department and you're not an official, so why should I listen to you?" That's the difference.

Statements by low-level managers certainly serve a purpose. However, they're often cruel to workers and the relationships are bad, so they cannot become workers' delegates.

During the strike, some common workers changed dramatically in terms of both their boldness and speaking ability. One female worker from the factory recently went to a new factory. She immediately took three workers with her to report their boss. I say this kind of thing cannot be wiped out. We just need to maintain the network.

Personal Experiences

I graduated from a vocational high school (*zhongzhuan*) in 1993 with a degree in civil engineering. The school was in my hometown and I was assigned to a township collective enterprise after graduation. We were the last class from our school to be assigned work placements. I worked on a construction site as a construction technician (*shigong jishuyuan*). I turned the diagrams into reality. Now we call that position project manager. When I had just graduated, my wage was low, just two or three hundred yuan per month. The economy was in rough shape. I wanted to find work that would pay immediately. I had no thought of starting my own business.

I worked there for several years, until 1997. The economy was weak, and there was a currency bubble that hit the real estate industry hard. I got married and had a child.

I had a dispute with the manager and secretary of our company. That was when our enterprise was still run in the manner of the old planned economy, so there was a target for materials. If we used twenty tons of steel on site but were issued twenty-five tons, we could sell the remaining five tons. When I had just gotten a job at the company, there were some procedures I wasn't familiar with and I fell into a trap someone had set. They asked me go to the Commodities Bureau and sign for the materials, so I went over and signed. But those materials had already been sold, and he just took the money and ran off. Later, a working group was sent by our superiors and stationed with us. When they discovered that I had signed, they asked me to explain. I went to find the secretary, but the secretary was in on it with the manager and wouldn't make a definitive statement. Those five tons of materials truly had nothing to do with me. Outraged, I left.

At that point, I sought out friends, moving first to Shaanxi, then to Liuzhou (Guangxi). I did construction work on highways and factories. We had to wait until construction was completed before we would be paid. I did that for several years, but I grew tired of it.

I arrived in Shenzhen in 2002 and paid a hundred yuan to an employment agency to get a job at a hardware factory that made springs and screws. The factory gave me a temporary residence permit. They held two months' wages at a time and there was a New Year's banquet but no bonus. At the time, I was only earning four hundred or five hundred yuan per month, and the other workers were about the same. I began in the factory as an apprentice, studying precision lathes. There were no days off at the factory. We didn't do overtime on Sunday, but every other day of the week we did. That was the first time I heard there was a minimum wage. There was a dormitory in the factory, but I rented an apartment. The food provided by the factory was decent, and on Sundays I could take the meal with me and eat with my wife.

In those days, people would sustain minor injuries at the factory, but no one had heard of compensation for such injuries. If you were injured, the management would just assign you to lighter duties. If a boss paid for your treatment when you were injured, that was a good boss. I don't know how much the boss made per year, but he was definitely bringing in some money because the second year he bought a small piece of land. He built a five-story factory and a seven-story dormitory on it. He also bought some brand new machinery. The boss had a military background, but he was in his thirties and had already retired.

All the workers were trained in the factory, and our wages were all low. Hardware factories are pretty grimy. The turnover is high. Some workers came, saw how bad the working conditions were, and immediately left.

Above the employees were the supervisors, and above them were the managers. The boss set the unit price and the supervisors organized production. They were also paid only a few hundred yuan per month, not much more than us. I had one manager who was in his twenties, younger than me.

My wage was based on a time rate when I started but later was changed to a piece rate. After I left the factory, I realized the unit prices the boss paid were unfair. He set them at whatever price he wanted. If you made more, he would lower the unit price. There was no scientific principle to it. It was difficult to resign from the hardware factory. I was pretty good with the machine and was on good terms with my supervisor, so the manager wanted me to stay and continue training. But when I told them I wanted to go to BBK Electronics [a major Chinese corporation], they approved my resignation. Other people had a hard time getting their resignations approved because it was hard to find workers in those days.

When I left that hardware factory, my cousin introduced me at BBK Electronics. That factory had a big name, but who knew that even doing such important work, the wages were still pitifully low? My job was to push a cart delivering partially completed products to the assembly line. There were eleven assembly lines and several thousand employees. The pay was 350 yuan per month with 1.1 times normal pay for overtime. It was terribly exhausting. There weren't even water breaks.

My hometown is still focused mainly on agricultural products like tea, tangerines, and oranges. Over the past few years, many people from my hometown have returned to look for work there. I'm the only one I know who's still working outside—everyone else went back. Some drive vehicles [to transport goods] in our hometown and others sell waste products. In general, people figure out some way to make a living, usually by doing some kind of retail business. Of course, there are also many people who work in factories. There's a cement factory, a lime plant, and a number of mines. There's also a factory that makes prefabricated boards. The pay there is two thousand yuan per month, and the managers aren't strict. When there's farming to do, people can go home and help out.

A cousin of mine worked as an agent in our hometown selling Geonee brand phones. He made more money than some people but less than others. Someone from my hometown opened a garment factory in Guangzhou. Later, he returned home and opened another, but it folded before long.

I forgot how to farm long ago. Now we're completely dependent upon the city. Going back to the village is just waiting to die.

An Employee from the Factory Warehouse

"Many workers' delegates got scared and refused to go back. I wasn't scared."

In 2001, I started working at a hardware factory run by a local boss. There were probably two hundred employees. The basic monthly wage was 350 yuan, including food and lodging. I met Mr. Wu while working at the injection-molding machine. Because he was educated, he was doing quality control for the factory. At the time, he struck me as well-spoken, and he could read diagrams. He never gambled or played cards, and he loved to read. I left that factory after eight months and later happened to get a job at the furniture factory. It was quite a coincidence that I ended up with Mr. Wu again.

When I began working there, in June 2004, there were more than 3,000 employees. I worked as a cook in the cafeteria. Before the 2013 strike, cooks earned 2,200 yuan per month, with no overtime. The boss disbanded the cafeteria in March 2013. Some of the cafeteria workers left, and others arranged to be transferred to the shop floor. I ended up operating a machine in the warehouse. It was simple—the training took less than half a day. At first I was unwilling to go to the shop floor, but because they work overtime there, their pay was a bit higher than in the cafeteria, around 2,900 yuan per month. The foremen's pay was 400 yuan per month higher than the workers' pay.

There were a lot of fines in the factory: one hundred yuan for spitting, two hundred yuan for smoking. In the past, the boss would frequently go onto the shop floor to catch people smoking. If you had perfect attendance for a month, you would receive an award of only sixty yuan, whereas if you took just one day off, you would be fined one hundred yuan. There were production quotas on the shop floor, and we couldn't punch out until we had completed them. Younger employees would play on their phones. They got yelled at if the managers caught them doing it. Some of the younger employees had long hair and earrings, even tattoos. There were also workers who got tattoos after being hired.

The Big Boss and the guards used to be rather brutal. While we were waiting in line for our meals, the guards would hit us if people didn't keep the line straight. It changed a lot over time, and the guards stopped hitting people. When I began at the factory, the surrounding area was desolate. Now it's booming. The local villagers keep putting up taller and taller buildings.

In 2006, the factory began to relocate. In total, we lost more than one thousand employees. The factory grounds started out quite large, but they were constantly being reduced. Some shop floors were shuttered. The guard room kept being moved further inward.

From the beginning of 2013 until the strike, they moved eight injection-molding machines from the factory. One day I walked out of the warehouse to get water and saw them moving a machine. Others had already gone on strike and were blocking the flatbed truck with the machine on it. The warehouse where I worked was in a different location than the other factory buildings, so I wasn't immediately aware of the strike. It wasn't until the fourth day that I joined them in blocking the truck. Workers ran up to scold us for continuing to work, so we stopped. The head of the engineering department, who was responsible for repairing the machines, also told us to turn off the air compressor. He said that the entire factory had stopped working. Only a few of us were still running the machines, wasting electricity.

I didn't attend the first negotiation. I heard that because the government personnel took video recordings during the negotiations, many workers' delegates got scared and refused to go back. I wasn't scared. What's more, I had been at the factory a long time and everyone knew me. That's why I attended the second round of negotiations. The negotiations were held at the labor station. There were eight workers' delegates and five factory and government representatives. In addition to the Big Boss, these included the bosses' lawyer, a manager, and two people from the labor station.

The Big Boss began by saying, "I have to get orders overseas. It's exhausting. You workers are my wealth, but right now is not the time because I'm broke. I'm also being treated for a severe cold." He said he had no intention of relocating the factory, but if workers were unwilling to work, he would give them four hundred yuan compensation per year worked. He asked, "Are you willing to work or not? Can you delegates even make that decision?"

I said, "That's not enough. We are just conveying the workers' opinions. We cannot represent the workers, we can only tell them what you've said and see whether they agree."

There was someone from the labor station present, and when he heard the Big Boss say he would pay only four hundred yuan [per year worked], he responded emphatically, "That's too little!" In general, the people from the labor station never got angry.

The Big Boss said, "I have to go get treated for my cold. Just go on talking with the lawyer." When he was about to leave, he looked back and said to us, "Each of you has to watch out for yourself" (*nimen yao ziji baohu ziji*). In total, we talked for about an hour before the Big Boss bowed out.

When we went to discuss things at the labor station that morning, many employees came and waited outside for an update. The general opinion was that at the very least we should be compensated according to the minimum monthly wage. When they heard the boss had offered only four hundred yuan, they just said, "No way. No way." There were people who wanted to go to the municipal government offices.

When the negotiations were over, I asked the workers to release the truck with the machine loaded on it. Management was paying nine thousand yuan per day in rental fees. The government also said that they had come to inspect the factory several times, and they knew that the boss wanted to relocate. They asked us to first release the truck in the factory and promised the government would make sure we were compensated. As workers' delegates, we thought at the time that because the boss had offered compensation at a rate of four hundred yuan per year worked, maybe he would soften a bit if we released the truck and we would have less trouble negotiating. We thought that would be a good bargaining method. We were also worried that we would anger the government if we didn't release the truck, and if they didn't help us sort it out, we'd have a hard time. So, we said to the workers, "Let's take a step towards them."

None of the eight workers' delegates agreed when the Big Boss said he would give us four hundred yuan. As for the release of the truck, the delegates unanimously agreed to release it, though many workers did not agree. Some people complained, "We're releasing the truck without even reaching an agreement with the boss."

Each of us workers' delegates told the workers about the release of the truck, but it was Mr. Wu who did most of the talking. He stood in the factory compound and spoke to everyone.

The day after the negotiations, the labor station sent us a questionnaire asking everyone to write how much compensation they were demanding. Some people wrote two thousand yuan, others wrote sixteen thousand, and still others wrote eighteen thousand.

We were seized while marching to the government office on the last day. Everyone went back to the factory after we were released. There we saw a notice that all workers who participated in the negotiations had been fired. We didn't even get our wages for the days we were on strike.

Mr. Wu left a deep impression on me. He explained the law one provision at a time. He even convinced the lawyer. Mr. Wu was quick to respond but not impulsive. He argued for justice, so of course people said he was nosey (*duoguan xianshi*).

I'm originally from Jiangxi. There the government wanted to convert farmland back into forest. I heard it was planning to use it to raise pandas. My family had a total of ten *mu*,[17] and we received two hundred yuan per *mu*. Later, the government set aside a piece of land and leveled it. They built new housing for residents.

Foreman Fu

"The boss is really shameless."

I left my village to work back in 1997. I got a job at a camera factory in Zhongshan with over one thousand workers, and I worked there for two or three years. The factory was in a new industrial district. The district government sent a factory director and a union chief. At that time, we got three yuan per hour of overtime and rice was still less than one yuan per *jin*.[18] There was a union in the factory, and the union chief was getting pretty old—around forty or fifty years old. At the time, the factory operated all year round and rarely hired new workers.

The factory celebrated workers' birthdays. They were once every two months or sometimes once every three months. Regular workers were given sunflower seeds, and the foremen were given shirts. The district government would select ten outstanding workers every year. I remember the award was two thousand yuan.

I remember one time there was an accident in a different department in the factory. An injection-molding machine malfunctioned and crushed a worker's hand. They weren't sure what to do, so they called the mechanic. It took more than an hour to get his hand out. They said the machine was off and told him to pull his hand out, but he wouldn't. He just stayed there screaming while a foreman held him. Finally, they opened up the machine. All that was left were pieces of his hand. It looked like a fishnet or something. It had been pulped. Later, everyone donated money for him.

I'm now forty-six years old. I worked at the factory for ten years, eight of those as a foreman. I participated in multiple negotiations as a workers' delegate. At the first negotiation after the strike was called, there were more men than women, and most of them were foremen. We spoke to the management in a harsh tone, such that there was nothing they could say. However, during the negotiations, they brought a camera and took photos of all the delegates. Only a few delegates were willing to return for the second round of negotiations because they feared retaliation.

Many of the delegates were different for the second round, and this time there were more women than men. In my opinion, the delegates at the second round did a poor job. They couldn't speak up to the management and were easily ignored. They were also the ones who agreed to release the truck. Mr. Wu participated in all the negotiations and never dropped out.

Several so-called advocacy lawyers (*weiquan lüshi*) came to assist the workers, but they left a bad impression on me. They began by saying there was no basis for the workers' demand for compensation. They argued that because the factory hadn't yet finished moving the machines, there was no way we would be compensated. We were upset to hear that and didn't contact them again. The lawyer for the factory was a woman. She was too showy. During the negotiations, the bosses' lawyer often manipulated the labor station director's words.

I thought the director of the labor station was all right. It seemed like he was really helping the workers. Before the negotiations, he gave us some ideas and told us how to talk to the management. I heard that in the past, this director had fined bosses for illegal activities. I heard that once, when a boss was withholding wages, the director asked him to come over and talk it through, but the boss didn't want to go. The director said, "Come on, there's nothing to worry about." When the boss finally went, some workers beat him up. As a result, the boss quickly came up with the money and paid the workers everything he owed them.

The management also invited another lawyer to the negotiations. We kept him there until two thirty in the morning because he wouldn't negotiate honestly with us. With all those workers waiting outside, he was afraid to leave. Later, he said he was quitting and didn't want the boss's money. He said he was never going to take on that kind of labor dispute again because it was unbearable.

Mr. Wu was too honest and inflexible. I knew of him in the factory, but we didn't have much contact. I also knew that he distributed flyers in the factory with information about fighting for our rights. During the strike, we often urged Mr. Wu not to show his face during worker actions. Sometimes he listened to us, sometimes he didn't. When he was seized, it was because he didn't listen. When we were marching to seek an audience, several workers' delegates on the scene saw that the situation was bad when a group of police blocked the road. They left and called out to Mr. Wu, telling him to "disappear." Unconcerned, he continued to march with the workers. Then several hundred Special Police arrived and seized everyone.

When Mr. Wu was seized, a group of female workers surrounded him, trying to prevent the seizure, but they couldn't stop it. Ultimately, everyone was taken in. Mr. Wu was taken in a separate vehicle. Only one of the interrogated workers made a damaging statement about Mr. Wu. The police told him he had broken the law, and I guess he got scared and said Mr. Wu was the one who called for the march.

Two days before we were seized, we had agreed with management that negotiations would continue. I even heard someone from the management's side say that the maximum compensation would be sixteen hundred yuan. The problem was that those women kept shouting, and everyone followed them onto the streets. They were just a bunch of impulsive women from the countryside.

Why was the final result so terrible? There are two main reasons. First, because we released the truck and thus lost our main bargaining chip. We should never have released the truck, and we should have kept the private vehicles belonging to Boss Two and his secretary. They fooled us many times over. Second, because the boss was too lazy and had a history here.

Before the strike, there were two nearby factories where

the workers had also raised a ruckus when there were preparations for relocation. They blocked the gates for just two days and the problem was resolved. At one, the workers received sixteen thousand yuan per year worked in compensation, and at the other, they received compensation based on their average wage over the past twelve months. Those bosses had prepared funds. If they could have paid less, of course they would have. Right now, there are workers at another factory who've been occupying the factory for several days.

I haven't had much work since leaving the factory. Recently, I got a position at another factory. The work was twenty-six days per month and the wage was around 2,850 yuan, not counting overtime. But it was tedious work, so I left. Now it's hard to get a position in the big factories. I went to apply to one factory and they said they wouldn't hire me because they couldn't buy work-related injury insurance for workers over age forty-five. Right now, a lot of new factories are opening. The big emptied-out factory buildings from before are being rented to smaller factories. Each floor can be rented to several individual factories. I'm not willing to work for a small factory because they don't pay the legal overtime rate. They only give you nine yuan more per hour. It's nothing. So, I'm mostly relying on my wife right now.

I like to buy lottery tickets and play slot machines. My daughter is a freshman in college. She just started, and I still haven't gotten enough money together to pay her tuition.

Foreman Gong of the Bronzing Department

"We couldn't control the workers' emotions."

Before the Strike

I'm thirty-four years old this year. I come from Guangxi, where I graduated from junior secondary school. I moved to Shenzhen to find work in 2004 and began working at the factory in September of that year. I was working as a common worker when the management saw that I had a nimble mind and made me a foreman. Foremen didn't have much higher wages in those days, just one thousand yuan per month more. I left the factory in February 2006 to spend Chinese New Year in my hometown, then returned in March.

Before the strike, I was a foreman in the bronzing department on the second floor.

Those of us who were senior employees knew with certainty that they were relocating machinery. They moved machinery from the factory many times. We even took photos. I took photos with my phone, both when they disassembled the machine and when they loaded it onto a flatbed truck. Now all those photos have been deleted.

The boss also had a factory in Huizhou. I even went there to help out, so how could I possibly fail to notice that he was relocating the factory? Those of us who were technically proficient were sent to Huizhou because they were having some technical issues there.

At the beginning of 2012, the management moved several machines. They had hired many new employees the year before, but most of them stayed only a few months before resigning. There was a regulation in our factory that required one month's notice before someone could resign, but during those months, anyone who wanted to resign could just leave.

There was nothing to do on the day before the New Year, so we distributed red envelopes [with money in them, as holiday bonuses] and held an all-factory meeting. Boss Two told all the employees the factory would relocate that year, although it was possible that some sections would continue production in Shenzhen.

The management relocated machinery twice before the strike was called.

The factory orders were being sent to Huizhou. As a foreman, I was naturally aware of this. When the orders were received, they came to my desk. Employees who complained about having less overtime would come look over the orders on my desk. But then some of the orders that were given to me were never completed. Instead they were removed, so I knew the orders had been sent to Huizhou. It seems that the orders started going to Huizhou in March or April.

The boss was moving the machinery and said they would relocate, but he told us nothing else. Of course the employees felt uneasy; how could we not? Everyone was definitely upset, especially the senior employees.

Based on my experience in school, the strike seemed to me like raising money for a student field trip: everyone had to pay their share. During the strike, people had to stay hydrated, and there were various expenses that had to be paid, so before the strike began, each foreman (*zuzhang*) collected money from their work team (*zu*). There were only a few who didn't pay. Those who didn't pay in advance contributed once the strike was called. Each person had to pay at least ten yuan.

Before the strike, we said to the workers, "We're all advocating for ourselves now. Don't say who the workers' delegates are. Everyone represents himself or herself. During the strike, we will all say that there are no delegates and that each person represents himself or herself."

Before the strike, we foremen held a brief discussion. Mr. Wu reminded us not to tell the workers, because he worried someone would give away the secret. In truth, there was really no plan. We just agreed that when the management went to take a machine we would wait until it was loaded on the truck and then we would stop it from leaving.

We also heard people say that some strikes went on for several months with the employees just baking in the sun day after day, and how hard that was. It was especially hard for the leaders (*laoda*) who had to constantly urge everyone on. They had to convince people that it was all for their own good, and that they had to continue the struggle.

Even after working for many years, we would be left with nothing if the factory relocated. If we didn't fight for our interests before the relocation, it wouldn't matter if we went all the way to Huizhou to track down the boss—no one would listen to us.

On the day of the strike, they were moving machinery from the injection-molding department. The senior employees knew they would be taking the machinery that day. They'd been there a long time, so they knew what was going on. They knew it would happen on that day, but they didn't know the exact time.

Two machines, one big and one small, had already been moved to Huizhou before the strike began. The employees knew that if a few more machines were relocated, they would be able to begin production in Huizhou and everyone at the old factory would be let go. It was delayed for a few more months, but there was no overtime. At sixteen thousand yuan per month, many employees wanted to resign.

Conflict between the Workers and the Management

At nine thirty that morning, the crane loaded the injection-molding machines onto the truck. We came out from the shop floor to block the gate and stop it from leaving, and the strike had begun. Only a few workers continued working on the shop floor. On the second day, there were still people working. Each of the factory's four floors had a supervisor. None of the supervisors took part in the strike—they just stood there watching us. Some neutral foremen didn't come out, either. Instead they just sat on the shop floor, hanging out.

The supervisors didn't dare ask us to work. They stood with the boss and never with the workers. They never mentioned any perks (*fuli*) for the workers. Many factories have unions, but ours didn't even have that. When I first left my hometown to look for work, I started at a factory that had a union. They would give us a few perks, hold birthday parties and distribute gifts for New Years. That factory had all kinds of programs. But in this factory, we didn't even know about the township union office. Even the word "union" was unheard of among the workers.

Our supervisor called the foremen, but I didn't answer. He was often rude to us, so this time we paid him no heed. We had asked him about a wage raise in the past, but he always said, "How dare you ask for a raise when you're doing such a lousy job?" He was very harsh. Because he was so insistent, there was nothing we could say.

The boss wasn't there on the first day of the strike. It seems he came on the second day, but I'm not sure. Often his car was there, but no one knew where he had gone.

After the strike was called, Boss Two's secretary came down from the office building. Without knowing what was going on, she asked the workers to be good and return to work. She said things could wait until the boss got back to discuss them. The secretary seemed to have more power than the boss, because all the supervisors listened to her. She had few responsibilities in the past, but at that point the entire administration department worked under her.

Someone said the secretary was the boss's lover, but you can never know about that sort of thing. If you don't have proof, it's all just conjecture. She had a child out of wedlock, but who cares about people's private affairs? What matters is how she managed the factory.

There were a lot of us there. We said all kinds of things until we had chased her away. With so many people, whom should she listen to? We asked, "What's the point of working without overtime? It's not acceptable for us to work in Shenzhen for less than two thousand yuan per month, while you secretly relocate the machinery. You said you aren't relocating, so why is it being moved?" The factory was already basically empty.

Impressions of Mr. Wu

I didn't know Mr. Wu in the beginning. He was on the third floor and I was on the second. But I saw him not far from the factory gates distributing information about the Labor Contract Law. Later, I got to know him and sometimes I chatted with him when I went to the third floor.

Mr. Wu was a common worker who worked there day in, day out. Unlike us foremen, he was usually too busy to try and organize things. Moreover, what would you do if the supervisor saw you?

The workers felt discouraged for the first few days of the strike. Not even the government was listening to us. Mr. Wu was a good colleague and helped us foremen encourage everyone. After all, if we spoke to the workers, they would listen.

Some workers knew what was up. They said we definitely needed to hold together and that we needed delegates for when the boss came back to discuss things with us. The employees phrased it like this: we have the right to seize the boss's property. If he's going to take his property and go, what right do we have? We have no rights. Some workers understood things a bit better than leaders. If they thought about something, they would ask us to make arrangements.

During the first few days, Mr. Wu never spoke in front of a crowd. Later, during the negotiations, Mr. Wu served as a delegate. When the boss came and said he wouldn't negotiate with us, Mr. Wu saw how down everyone was feeling and consoled us. He sat together with the workers' delegates and said words of encouragement.

From then on, whenever someone from the Labor Bureau came, people would call out for Mr. Wu to come and have him do the negotiating.

One day, I saw police officers and labor dispute officers (*laodong jiucha*) ask for Mr. Wu. They said he was the only one the workers would listen to. Mr. Wu replied that he was not a foreman or a supervisor, so why would the employees listen to him? Those people still insisted that the employees listened to him. Mr. Wu said the employees didn't listen to him, they trusted him. In the early days, the police all acted the same way: they sought out Mr. Wu as soon as they arrived. Why did they want Mr. Wu specifically? Because they thought we would all listen to him. In those days, Mr. Wu often told the employees not to cause trouble or do anything inappropriate. The police thought he was our leader.

In truth, I believe most employees weren't conscious of the fact that he wasn't a foreman. I think that when it started, most employees didn't know him.

During those days, one of the workers who waited at the factory every day collapsed from a heart attack. I went to find a car to take him to the hospital.

The Police Officer Who Enraged the Masses

One time, a man came driving a police car and wearing a police uniform. He had a utility belt on, and it seemed he was carrying a gun. As soon as he arrived, he began angrily saying he represented the government and had come to resolve the issue. He asked for our delegates to come out and discuss it. We asked Mr. Wu to go, and Mr. Wu used both hands to respectfully hold out a piece of paper carrying the workers' demands. The cop ripped it out of his hands and threw it to the ground without looking at it, yelling, "You! Come back!"

Where in the world can you find such crazy cops? Aren't they supposed to serve the people? He seemed to be serving himself. Who cares if he had a gun? We weren't afraid because we hadn't broken the law. He was alone. If he had been so bold as to try firing the gun, with so many of us, we would have killed him.

Everyone was upset, so we surrounded him and demanded an apology. We asked him, "Is this how the government serves the people? Are you even from the government?" He hid in the office building. Later, he tried to climb the factory wall to escape, but he wasn't able to.

In the beginning we wondered whether he had been sent by the boss to intimidate us. Afterward, when we saw the chief of police, we asked whether that guy was really a cop. We said, "If you hired a gangster and gave him a gun, that's not right."

The police chief said, "I'll go talk to him."

The Gangsters Come

When the Labor Bureau came, they confused us. We didn't know which department they were from. The first people to come weren't wearing uniforms. One said he was something or other, but none of us knew what that meant. They came first, then called some gangsters to join them. The gangsters followed behind, wagging their tails. We stayed united and didn't allow them to enter. They also refused to show their credentials. That day we were a little overenthusiastic and didn't let them enter. Even if it were a secret investigation, they would have to let us know.

I forgot what exactly happened that day. Those people brought clubs and pitchforks. We said, "We're not raising a ruckus here. It's best if you don't come in." Then we blocked the road and didn't let them enter. It may have been a Shenzhen Patrol Force (*xunfangdui*) or something. They were all in disarray.

Some weren't even in uniform, but they were carrying clubs. I said we weren't going to fight. After all, we weren't causing problems, we were just standing up for our rights. We hadn't hit the boss and we hadn't touched a single box in the factory. We hadn't smashed any of the boss's property. We hadn't even moved anything. We were just blocking the truck without harming it. That day around twenty of them came. We said, "It's best if you don't come in. We won't stand for you coming in and beating people. There are two or three hundred of us here who will fight back. We're not attacking anyone, so what are you carrying those things for? If we were holding sticks and you came to suppress us, the police would come and it would all be over. But right now, none of the employees is holding anything."

I heard there was a woman in the administration department who paid them, and that an employee saw it happen. I didn't see it, but for them to show up, they certainly were paid. They were there to intimidate the workers—or at least see if they could intimidate the workers a little. Once they'd received the money, they left. They stood around the gates for more than half an hour before leaving. That was before the Big Boss came.

Later, the Big Boss did come. When he was explaining the situation to us, he said, "You just keep working hard, as usual, and we will not relocate." He said they were just moving one machine.

I said, "How can you neglect to mention all those machines you moved last year? We wouldn't have spoken up if you were just moving one, but now the whole shop floor has been emptied." There were so many of us that the boss fled. He ran off and didn't come back.

Selecting Delegates to Negotiate

They began to come by often to negotiate. They would immediately ask us to choose delegates. I said, "The employees are all afraid that you'll chase the delegates off or pay them to run off. Then what would we do? We would be left with no delegates."

That's what all the employees were privately thinking. If you seven or eight people went, and the boss paid each of you ten thousand yuan, you would leave and then what would the remaining employees do? The boss would ignore us and the government would ignore us, and then what would we do to keep from starving? That's how the employees saw it.

But they made us choose delegates anyway. They said it would be impossible to communicate if we all spoke at once—the boss could only say two sentences before getting overwhelmed. With so many people, it was hard to unify our opinions. The people from the Labor Bureau came every day. They said they too were unable to resolve the issue because the boss said he wasn't relocating the factory. That was the only answer they would give us. Finally, two people wearing uniforms came, but I don't know where they were from. The tall one had an armband labeled "Labor Dispute Officer," so obviously he was from the Labor Bureau.

I didn't participate in the first negotiation. I only went for the later ones.

During that round, the boss said, "With all of you speaking at once, I can't understand a word you say. I don't know how to talk to you. You have to choose some delegates."

The Labor Bureau and the police station said the same thing, that it was impossible to fit three hundred people in an office.

One employee said, "We don't have delegates, so we'll go in one by one."

The Labor Bureau personnel said, "We can't allow each of you to come in. That might be possible in the Great Hall of the People, but you can't all squeeze into this office."

If we went in, you know, the police were afraid we would destroy property. They worried the employees would get worked up and something would happen.

In the end, we chose eight delegates. Two middle-aged women and Mr. Wu were common workers, and the other delegates were foremen. Mr. Wu probably went to every round of negotiations. When the employees started urging him to step forward, he was a little reluctant to go, but whoever the employees called on went. The two women who were chosen as delegates had been working at the factory for many years. There were also people who said it would be fine if only the foremen went.

The workers' delegates we selected asked the remaining foremen to watch the employees. It wouldn't do to have the employees raising a ruckus or breaking things.

After negotiations broke down, the people from the police station and the Labor Bureau saw Mr. Wu speaking to the workers. There was always someone nearby watching our every move. People from the police station took photos with their cell phones as some kind of evidence. Each and every one of our movements was recorded.

The first few days were rather calm. We were at it so long that the sun had darkened our skin.

When we were in the factory having a drink of water, the boss's secretary cut the power. What if we drank unboiled water and got diarrhea? We said to the police, "They're so stingy about this little bit of electricity!" We personally bought water so we wouldn't have to drink a drop of the management's water. Some of the employees had stomach issues and felt queasy when drinking cool water. I said to the police, "We've been striking all these days and you haven't worked on the issue at all. Regardless of how powerful a boss is, the government has the ability to put pressure on him, yet the government is taking his side while so many workers have to sit around waiting for their next meal." Some workers had three family members depending on them.

As soon as people from the government or the Labor Bureau came to the factory, it was always common workers or us foremen who surrounded them and started speaking. It was never Mr. Wu. But once we selected delegates to negotiate, they often saw Mr. Wu talking openly with us. They saw him sitting in the center or in some prominent position. It was apparent that employees really listened to him, so those official personnel always sought him out. Sometimes they forced him to come out.

We discussed things before the negotiations and printed out our demands so we could present them clearly to the boss. The document said, "Because the boss is secretly relocating the machinery, the employees are too anxious to focus on their work. Therefore, the employees present the following demands . . ."

The first demand was for monetary compensation. The boss said he could not respond to this demand. The second related to the high-temperature subsidies. Finally, there were the pensions. When he responded to the latter two issues, I said those were the minor items. The first one was the most important. He had not addressed the important point, so I asked again that he address it.

The boss couldn't refuse to do something the Labor Bureau required him to do, right? The pensions, for example: if the workers asked him to pay into the pension program, he couldn't refuse. The boss responded that, yes, he could pay into the pension program for the past several years. But we didn't have the money for our contributions. Each of us would have to pay more than ten thousand yuan.

On the third day of the strike, the Big Boss came out once and was intimidated. After that he only came to speak with us once at the Labor Bureau, and he didn't stay more than a few minutes. Without discussing the issues, he just told us to speak with his lawyer. He said he didn't need to talk to us. He began by stating the compensation would be three hundred yuan per year worked, and the delegates told him that was unacceptable. That's when the boss said he had a cold and bowed out. The factory director was there, and he said the boss really was sick and couldn't take part in the talks. Then the lawyer began to talk, talk, and talk some more, until we had finally reached five hundred yuan. By then the employees, many of whom were waiting outside for news, were starting to get worked up. They had started out full of hope. Who knew that the Big Boss would run off almost as soon as he'd come and that we'd never see him again? Seeing that the Big Boss left after just a few minutes, it was obvious nothing had been accomplished. Later, the workers' delegates came out and said the most they could get was five hundred yuan.

I didn't go to the first negotiation with the Big Boss, but I went to the later meetings with Boss Two. The secretary often came down to plead with us. She posted an announcement on the wall for us to read. It said they were going to buy pensions, that we should bring copies of our identity cards. The employees thought, "I've worked here five or six years, maybe even seven or eight. How much money would that be?"

The Labor Bureau told us that the boss wasn't relocating the factory. They asked us to release the truck and return to work. Mr. Wu also urged everyone to release the truck. At that point, some people blamed Mr. Wu. I said, "You're the ones who selected these people, and now you want to complain."

Later, the boss had another truck come to take away molds. Some employees were so angry they let the air out of the tires.

The government urged us to go through labor arbitration, and the Labor Bureau sent people to investigate the factory. They asked things like whether wages were being withheld and whether the overtime rates were legal. The employees feared that the Labor Bureau personnel would use the investigation to take important documents from the factory, so they stopped the inspectors from entering and demanded to see what they were carrying.

Petitioning at the Government Offices

The first time workers were detained, I managed to escape. Once the township government seized us, we began urging workers not to approach the township government offices. But everyone exclaimed, "The township government just detained us that one time, and now they don't even care that we're blocking the road. We have to go to the municipal government."

The day before we went to the municipal government to petition, a bespectacled man came to the factory. He was a clerk, but I can't remember if he worked for the government or the Labor Bureau. He came to the factory to warn us not to do anything untoward, because that day everyone was calling for people to march to the government offices. In the end, we'd already done so many things, marching one day, doing a sit-in the next day, marching somewhere else the following day . . . that they often sent people to follow us.

We carried a banner during the march. It had something about a "black-hearted boss" written on it. In the past, some of the banners were handwritten, but workers said that those tore easily, so they asked several of us delegates to go to a press and print out a banner with a red background and white letters. I was in charge of that.

Early that day, some employees came looking for me and asked me to bring out the banner. They said they wanted to march immediately to the municipal government. I asked, "Why would you do that? Even if you marched all day, you wouldn't make it there before dusk." I urged them not to go. I also spoke to Mr. Wu and asked him to tell them not to go. I told them it wasn't like when China has a disagreement with a foreign country and it just goes out and does something.

Nevertheless, some of the workers left for the municipal government right away. They were really excited. They said, "Let's go have dinner there!" I said there might not be any dinner. Several women proclaimed that anyone who didn't go was a traitor.

Before we left the factory gates, I said to them, "You won't be able to find the government offices. Even if you do, it won't be until evening, after the sun has set. Everyone will be off work, and then who'll you talk to?" One worker said, "Can't we wait there? We've been waiting for days."

Mr. Wu didn't want to go that day, but he was thinking of the workers. He worried that something would happen to everyone on the road, so he went with them. He didn't do it for himself. Come to think of it, I remember one time, after the negotiations concluded, I heard that the boss wanted to bribe Mr. Wu 110,000 yuan to drop the case. Mr. Wu is an incredibly honest man. If he were doing it for himself, he would have taken the money and left. He never got agitated during the investigations, staying calm the whole time. I've been to his home, and it's modestly furnished. He also has several family members to think about.

Mr. Wu never encouraged people to do those things. The march, the sit-in, and the march to the municipal government that day—none of them were his idea. He said from the beginning, "If you want to go to the government offices, we can do that, but we can only send seven or eight people. Send delegates with a letter from the workers and a list of demands."

The employees said seven or eight people would not be enough, that there's power in numbers. We had sent five or six people, sometimes even seven or eight, to all the government departments many times and nothing had worked. We had submitted our list of demands, but they had just set them aside. Some offices wouldn't even accept them. After the delegates came back, there was no word from the offices. At most, they would delay or pass responsibility on to someone else. One time when we went to the police station, a police chief told us that these matters weren't under his control, that they concerned a different chief. When we went back to ask again, the original police chief was out on a business trip. He was purposefully leading us on. As it went on, the workers got more and more worked up.

On the road to the government office, the riot police followed us constantly. There were also people from the police station and the Labor Bureau following us. When we left the township, they stopped following us and people from a different Labor Bureau and a different police station took over. On the way, they were constantly urging us to go back. No one listened. There was a section of the highway missing, and that's where the armed police ran up to the front of our group. They blocked our path and then surrounded us. They started pushing us toward the gap in the road. Some employees didn't comply, so the armed police began to hit them. A woman from our group threw a lunch box at the armed police and the Special Police seized her. A cop from our township pointed at Mr. Wu and said, "There he is! There he is!" Then several Special Police attempted to seize him. Workers linked their arms in front of Mr. Wu in an effort to stop them, but the Special Police dragged him into a van. Every one of us was seized.

Conclusion

Some people were hospitalized. Some were beaten and others weren't. After walking for more than three hours, we may just have been exhausted. I heard that, at the hospital, one of the workers was so upset she tried to jump from the window.

When they were taking my confession, an officer from the Special Police asked where I was from. I said I was from Guangxi, and he said his girlfriend was also from Guanxi. I said, "You don't need to tell me about that . . ."

Enraged, he shouted, "Sit!" I said I wouldn't. He said, "I tell you to sit and you don't sit. . . . Then sit on the floor!"

I said, "Why should I listen to you? I haven't broken any laws."

They asked me who the leaders were and how many there were. I said that there were no leaders. Each of us personally wanted to go to the municipal government, probably two hundred of us. Then they asked me about the fire that broke out in the factory and whether or not we had started it. I said, "How would I know? I was at my apartment when the fire broke out."

Later, they gave me a typed document and had me sign with fingerprints. About ten copies were printed. I asked to have a look but they wouldn't let me. They said I had to sign quickly with all ten fingers.

My statement was only a few sentences, but they printed out a long document and then used my hand to sign it. I still don't know what was written in it.

They released me the next day. Those who carried the banner were held for seven days, and there were also two workers who were held for more than a month. One was the woman who was photographed throwing a lunch box at the police. The other was a man who led us in chanting slogans. He had a loud voice and was tall. On the road we shouted, "Black-hearted boss!" I don't know why Mr. Wu was held for so long.

We couldn't control the workers' emotions. We told them at the time that blocking the road wouldn't work. We said we'd tried it before, and we couldn't keep trying it again and again. The first time the Special Police seized us was already unnerving.

The last time we were taken to the police station, a police chief who had walked with us for three hours said, "Look at yourselves. You walked for three hours, and you forced me to walk three hours with you. Enough is enough. Squat down and don't move! And you still expect us to feed you?"

We also asked the NGO for advice, and they said: One, don't do anything too militant. Two, use microblogs to tell people about what has happened and attract more attention. As long as you don't do anything too radical, outside observers will support you.

Bronzing Department Worker Ms. He

"The main issue is that the government deceived us."

I started at the factory in 2008. I worked in the bronzing department on the second floor. I had never seen the Big Boss before the strike was called.

Boss Two told the entire staff he wanted to relocate the factory because a subway station was going to be built on the factory site. Boss Two said they would move to a new location in Shenzhen, though a specific site had not been confirmed. But we all knew there was a subsidiary plant in Huizhou. The boss had moved machinery to Huizhou in the past. The fourth floor had been emptied and half of the first floor was relocated.

On the first day of the strike, an employee, it seems it was a cleaner, came up to the second floor to notify us. He said that the first floor had gone on strike. When we went to the windows to look down, we saw that the management was moving machinery. After that, no one had any intention of working, and we all went down together. The third-floor supervisor had two in-laws employed there, as did the fourth-floor supervisor. None of the four of them participated in the strike. There were also some girls in the factory who continued to work while we were on strike.

We sat in front of the office building and waited for the boss to speak with us. The management closed the shop floor. No employees were allowed to enter. When we started getting drinking water from the security office, the management cut the power so we wouldn't have hot water.

I took part in the first round of negotiations. Three people from the boss's side came, and there were representatives from the township government and the police department. The work-

ers' delegates stood there, hardly saying anything. The whole discussion lasted less than five minutes. Boss Two refused to admit
that the relocation was happening and left. The representatives of
the government said they needed to investigate the matter.

The Big Boss came several days later. I remember it was
raining that day. Standing before a corrugated iron building,
he asked us, "Who said we're relocating?" We said, "Boss Two
did." The Big Boss said, "Well, we're not moving. It's been delayed two years. Go back to work."

We didn't believe him, so we said, "They're moving all the
machines from the factory. How will we keep working with no
machinery?" That's when the Big Boss left.

When the strike had just begun, the other older women
and I surrounded anyone from the government or from management who came to the factory. We would give them an ear-
ful, and they began asking us to select workers' delegates.

At some point, a person drove to the factory. We didn't
know what he was doing there. Stepping out of his car, he said
he was a government representative come to resolve the issue.
Everyone began speaking at once, so he asked us to choose a
delegate. We asked Mr. Wu to act as a delegate. Many people
still didn't know Mr. Wu at that point. When the strike was
called, I only knew him by his nickname; it wasn't until recently that I learned his full name. During the negotiations,
we asked Mr. Wu to speak on behalf of the workers because he
expressed himself clearly.

Mr. Wu sometimes stood on a platform to speak to us.
He said, "We have to be united. We need to fight together for
compensation." He didn't volunteer to speak. He only spoke up
because the workers asked him to.

The government cheated us twice. The first time was when
they guaranteed that the boss would negotiate with us if we
released the truck and let them take the machinery. The boss
was anxious about the truck because it was rented. A person
from the government said that the daily rental fee for the truck

was expensive, five thousand yuan per day. The people from the government even wrote a contract (*zizhu*), but when we asked them to sign it, they said there were no stamps they could use. They asked the workers to trust that the government would not deceive them. Though we were reluctant to let the truck go, we released it because we didn't want to get on the government's bad side. Even then, the boss still wouldn't negotiate with us.

The second time we were cheated was when the factory director brought an American customer from Huizhou. The American spoke Chinese, but we didn't know why he was there. The factory director told the workers' delegates that the factory would not relocate. He even demanded we compensate the factory for damages caused by their inability to ship orders. So, we stopped the factory director from leaving. The government people came to the scene and again guaranteed (*dabaopiao*) that they would come back to the factory the next day to negotiate. Ultimately, they did not come the next day.

The strike dragged on for a long time, but what's important is that the government deceived us when we asked for assistance.

The night before we went to the city, many workers debated whether or not to march. It was all older women and men who participated in those discussions. Mr. Wu didn't want people to go to the municipal government, but we departed at eight o'clock the next morning. Some older women there scolded people, saying, "Whoever doesn't go today is a traitor. You have to go, or the boss isn't going to compensate you." I saw that Mr. Wu didn't want to go, but those female workers berated him into coming out. He had no choice.

The sun was scorching that day. On the road to the municipal government, we got very thirsty. I began to cry. I said to the Special Police bringing up the rear, "You all have parents. Would you stand for it if your parents were out there being bullied?" One officer took out the water he had brought for himself and gave me some.

When we had walked halfway, the police surrounded us at an intersection on the high-speed road. Mr. Wu told everyone to sing revolutionary songs. Then the police seized everyone. I was held for ten days. When they took my confession, they asked me, "Do you know this person?" I said, "I do." They pressed my fingerprints on the document and had me sign some other documents I hadn't read.

Extrusion Department Worker Mr. Jiang

"Some delegates spoke often about how we had to obey the law—excessively so."

Regarding the Factory

When our factory was at its peak, there were a few thousand employees. People say the boss got his start as a gangster in Hong Kong and opened a small factory on the mainland in the 1990s. The Big Boss first opened a factory in Shandong, but the climate was too cool for high-temperature production, so they moved to Huizhou. The factory that's now in Huizhou was built with the boss's own money. Boss Two is the younger brother of the Big Boss, and they have a female secretary who usually takes care of everything in the factory. The legal owner is a woman. They say she's the former wife of the local village head. The chief of the Labor Bureau is apparently her younger sister or her brother-in-law. Below the boss there were supervisors, then assistant managers, then foremen.

I got a job at the factory in 2004, then quit in 2005 and returned home. I helped someone with construction, doing carpentry work. That same year I returned to the factory, and I've continued working there until today. The factory rotates workers between day shifts and night (*liang ban dao*). Wages are calculated by the hour. A portion is paid in cash and the rest is deposited into your bank account. They don't give you wage slips unless you ask. The factory had several departments including an extrusion department and an injection-molding department. We had three work teams (*zu*) in the extrusion department.

Before 2007, there were bonuses for perfect attendance,

but these stopped after 2007. The dormitories were free—all you had to pay was thirty yuan for utilities. Still, few people lived at the factory. Meals were provided in 2004, but in 2008 wages were raised to 900 hundred yuan per month, and meals were no longer provided. Instead, we paid a 270-yuan monthly fee for three meals a day. Now they've switched over to meal tickets that cost five yuan each. When the basic wage was raised, everyone went from working one machine to two. A point system was implemented with serious deductions for any misconduct. For every point deducted, there was a fine of five yuan. Boss Two often caught people smoking in the bathroom and fined them one hundred yuan each time. Year-end bonuses were awarded based on number of years worked: two hundred yuan for one full year worked and one hundred additional yuan for every year after that, with a maximum of six hundred yuan. Last year they canceled the year-end bonuses. Before the strike, wages ranged from around twenty-five hundred to three thousand yuan per month.

There were yearly physical examinations at the factory, which we had to pay for ourselves. The hospital would send personnel over to test things like blood pressure and heart and lung functions. There were also injuries in the factory. The boss compensated workers twelve thousand yuan for a finger injury.

It was usually quite hot in the shop floor. There were fans but no air conditioning. None of us knew there was supposed to be a subsidy for high-temperature work. During the strike, the workers' delegates demanded a five-hundred-yuan high-temperature subsidy, which the boss later gave us. He also compensated us for the previous year's paid leave and high-temperature subsidy. I didn't graduate from second grade of primary school, so I didn't understand anything about the law until delegates brought up such things during the strike.

There were no strikes in the factory before, but there were small disputes. Around 2009, there were six or seven young people from Henan who often got into fights. They would start fights in the cafeteria. At some point, they started a strike in the shop floor and said they would beat anyone who worked. The boss met their demands but later got rid of them one by one.

The guards used to be terribly arrogant. In 2004, they frequently beat people. If someone cut in line at the cafeteria, for example, the guards would shout at them and take their card. They were even ready to call a group of guards with their walkie-talkies to come and assault people. Also, if workers came back late after the New Year's holiday, the guards wouldn't let them back into the factory. Later, it progressed to the point that the guards had gangsters patrolling outside the factory. In the end, the head of security had his ankles stomped on. Afterward, the guards became more well-behaved. Inside the factory, the guards had the boss's support, but if they got into fights outside, the boss wasn't interested. If a guard made trouble off campus and was beat up, the boss would force him to leave. I heard that the Huizhou factory is about the same as Shenzhen was back in 2005, that the guards there still beat people.

In 2006, one worker went to another shop floor to pick up materials. The Big Boss happened to be patrolling, and when he saw the employee, he accused him of goofing off. The employee talked back, and the boss asked, "I'll beat the shit out of you—do you believe me?" The boss then assaulted the worker, but nothing came of it [that is, the worker didn't seek revenge or register a complaint].

People used to steal things from the factory. Once someone stole six wooden crates worth two hundred yuan each. At the time, our wage was only seven hundred yuan per month. That person was discovered and ran off without collecting his pay.

After the Sichuan earthquake, the factory did two donation drives. The first was voluntary, the second mandatory. Our supervisor hailed from Sichuan. He set the amount: a minimum of twenty yuan from each employee, deducted directly from our pay. I don't know where it all went.

The 2008 crisis didn't affect our orders, but many factories in Shenzhen closed. Over time, the factory's operations were standardized and improvements were made in many areas.

After the 2013 Chinese New Year, Boss Two held an all-factory meeting. He said he was going to relocate to Huizhou. Those who were willing could go with him, and those who weren't could collect their wages. At the beginning of the year, there were already just four hundred workers left, half of the number there were five years before. Few of the workers were born after 1990, and most of the women were over thirty years old.

The Strike

The day that we called the strike was the third time the boss moved machinery. We all knew about the previous two times, but no one took action.

Two days before the strike, the wife of an assistant manager, who was also a worker, went to the shop floor to collect signatures and ten yuan per person. I asked what she was doing, and she said, "We're going to have a strike. We need to buy drinking water, right? It will probably take more than one or two days, so we need to pool our money." As soon as I heard that, I put in my share. I didn't find it surprising or unreasonable, but there were some people unwilling to contribute money at that point.

The glass department led the strike. That day, the boss rented another big flatbed truck plus a crane to move the machinery from our shop floor. They loaded up several machines, but still no one in our department took action. People from the Glass Department came to our shop floor to deliver materials. That's probably when they noticed the machinery being moved. Our foreman told us they were striking outside, so we all went out—except for the foreman himself, who waited on the shop floor. He also asked us to tell the night shift not to enter the shop floor, since the supervisor was present, so they'd be asked to start the machines.

The crane was rented by the hour. A few days after we had

blockaded the vehicles inside the factory grounds, the crane's driver ran up and tried to force his way through. When we said, "You'll have to crush our bodies to drive out," he gave up.

The only reason the Big Boss showed up was that we had stopped the rented vehicles from leaving. He spoke with several of our delegates, and they told us, "The boss has agreed to compensate us four hundred yuan. We'll show him that we're negotiating in good faith and then continue until we've reached sixteen thousand yuan." They said that in order to show that we were sincere, we first needed to release the vehicles. There were workers who opposed this move, but the delegates were our backbone and we all had a great deal of confidence in them. The boss had come rushing to the scene. We didn't know the specifics of what they had discussed, except that the delegates said he had agreed to negotiate. Who knew that as soon as we released the vehicles, the boss would turn his back on us?

During the strike, we watched over the factory and stationed people at the gates. At night, we had workers watch the machines. The watch went until one o'clock in the morning, and we provided them bread to eat. I forgot what day, but there was a man, more than forty years old, who came to the factory in a police uniform, driving a police car. As he was driving up, he said, "I represent the people's government. You can tell me your demands." He asked us to select delegates to speak with him. Mr. Wu gave him our written demands, turned, and left. Without looking at them, the officer grew angry and yelled at Mr. Wu, "Come back!" like he was going to seize him. Mr. Wu said he wasn't a delegate. Everyone was angry, so we surrounded the police officer to prevent him from leaving. He was trapped in the factory. Three times he tried to climb the wall but wasn't able to get over it, though none of us pulled him down. We asked Mr. Wu to speak to him again because no one else was willing to. The two of them spoke in the office for a long time, and the officer wrote a guarantee that the issue would be resolved. The officer even said he "had a terrible fever." Really, he just wanted to get out of there, so we let him go. I called the government hotline 12345 to ask whether or not he was really from the government. I was worried the boss hired him to hoodwink us.

Another day, we were hanging out in the factory when I heard someone say that gangsters had come. I went to look and discovered there were around a dozen unidentified people at the factory gates. I didn't see any weapons, but I'm sure they had come prepared. There were a lot of us, so they took one look and left. I've seen this kind of thing in my hometown as well: armed thugs coming to assault people but then leaving before anything happens.

One day, there was a fire in the factory. The reporters, who had never come when we called before, now rushed over to see the fire. We told a reporter about the strike, but he just kept asking if we had started the fire. Later, I heard that the news report only covered the fire without a single word about our strike. When the fire started, the guards kept people outside and wouldn't let workers get close. There was no use in trying to file a police report—the police would stop listening as soon as they knew it was workers from our factory calling. By the time the firefighters showed up, the building had just about burned to the ground.

During the strike, there was a man from Henan who was constantly complaining. He opposed it when the workers' delegates released the truck, saying we should go out petitioning and demonstrating at government offices. He took part in the night shifts watching the gates, but he also drove an unlicensed motorbike taxi to make some extra money. He believed the workers should go out and make money when they weren't on call, but the workers' delegates argued everyone had to stick together and could not disperse. When they released the truck, the man from Henan scolded them. I don't know if it was the Henan man who drove the motorbike, but someone said, "What good is just waiting when we can go make some money?" Still, almost no one went out to make money during the strike.

The whole time, the clerks were just sitting in the office building with nothing to do. They came to the windows to look down on us when we were shouting in the yard. Later, the management had them go to the shop floor and work. The work wasn't technically demanding, so no training was necessary.

One day, we surrounded the legal representatives in the office building. We held them there for several hours, but we let them leave when the workday ended. It was mostly women who surrounded the office building. They said, "We don't even have food to eat. Are we going to let the boss eat as he deals with us?" Everyone agreed with this sentiment.

Negotiations

At the first meeting with the boss, we had eight delegates, including both foremen and common workers. The Big Boss told us all to go back to work. The delegates replied, "Are you kidding me? We've been on strike for so long." On a different occasion, he addressed a crowd of workers, telling everyone to return to work and promising they would not relocate for the time being. The workers demanded that he move the machines back, and he said he couldn't. The workers were furious. The boss responded that when we talked over one another, he couldn't understand what we were saying. He said, "You have to select delegates to speak with me." There were police on site at the factory during those discussions. No one derided the boss, nor did anyone threaten his safety. There was money in his pockets, but we weren't going to take it.

Each time the workers gathered together, it was Mr. Wu who did the talking. When the workers' delegates led a sit-in at the government offices, Mr. Wu stayed in the factory. He reminded us over the phone that it was just a sit-in, and that we were not to block the road.

There were more than a hundred of us who took part in the sit-in at the township government offices. Mr. Wu didn't go. He stayed at the factory. The government came out and said we were breaking the law, and then the police arrived and seized us. That day we were there until ten o'clock at night. Later, the government gave us water. During the sit-in, some people got scared when they saw the government coming toward us. Mr. Wu said, "Don't cause any chaos. Just sit there and don't commit any crimes." Most importantly, he understood the law. He said not to do anything unreasonable because he understands the legal system. If he came out now and took up the fight, there would still be many people there standing with him, myself included.

Our delegates always urged us not to argue and to be reasonable. I generally had little contact with the delegates. I knew they also worked at the factory, but I didn't know their names. I only got to know them during the strike, and for the rest of my life I will never forget them. Personally, I greatly admire Mr. Wu. After the strike, I had a meal with him and three foremen.

Thinking back now, during the strike I was like a club that struck wherever the delegates told me to strike.

Some delegates spoke often about how we had to obey the law, but I think we were too compliant with the government. Excessively so.

Visiting the Government Offices

On the last day when we marched together to the municipal government, we met the riot police on the road. Ultimately, three people were formally detained (*xingju*). One was a female worker who had thrown food at a "black skin" (defense force member). After they seized her, they said she had "assaulted an officer." That woman always had food with her when we were watching over the factory, so she also had a meal with her when we took to the streets.

We thought they wouldn't beat women, so we decided to have women march in the front. There were a lot of women, and most were thirty to fifty years old.

After I was seized, I thought about whether or not I would continue striking after my release. They didn't beat people in the police station. The police just questioned me. For half an hour, they asked whether I was striking of my own accord or whether someone had instigated it. They didn't ask about Mr. Wu. I said it was of my own free will. I had carried the banner in the march, so when the police pointed at a photo and asked if it was me, I said yes. They used a computer to document my confession and printed it for me to read. I just signed with my fingerprint without reading it. I'm uneducated, so I wouldn't understand the words even if I had read it. The police who interrogated me were reasonable—it was just the village's private security guys (*zhi'an zai*) who guarded us that had bad attitudes. The ten people who were marching at the front were all held for ten days. On the last day when they surrounded us, some of those in the front tried to break free. They were beaten and held for a longer period. My wife and I didn't fight. I was also at the front, and I would have been up there knocking heads if my wife hadn't stopped me. I'm pretty good in a fight. The government photographed everyone who was standing in front.

What left the deepest impression on me was how they acted when they seized us, as if we were bandits.

Taken to the Police Station

In the police station, the police cried, "Everyone sit down! You act like we're celebrating New Year!"

The food in the station was terrible. The rice stuck in your throat and the cabbage was barely even boiled before it was fed to us. I was starving and still I couldn't choke it down. During the ten days I was held, I quickly lost the fat on my stomach. I didn't even have a paunch when I got out. The weight loss program is free of charge in there. There were two of us workers to a cell. Other people were held in there as well: drug addicts, thieves, and drivers without licenses. There was also one who was injured from a fight. One kid even tried to swindle me.

In the end, some people were beaten and many people were detained. Everyone was frightened.

Many people were released the evening after we were seized. Some among those who got out recommended collecting money to hire Mr. Wu a lawyer. There were people, not sure how many, who didn't put any money up. Those people are heartless. In the end, we collected more than two thousand yuan. Now I fear we can't save him and that I'll be taken in again.

Many of us are still together, but we have no one like Mr. Wu to lead us. When we signed the evidence forms at the end, many people were unwilling to come. They were scared.

People worried that even if they continued to raise a ruckus, there would be no way to secure Mr. Wu's release and they too be thrown in with him. After the beatings, everyone was scared. We were a weak group. Coming to work isn't the same as fighting.

My cousin who started a small factory in Dongguan told me he is close with the police station there. Our boss is in here deep—that goes without saying.

Conclusion

I was in a high efficiency department with little waste. This was because we were practiced and the managers understood production. The Huizhou plant's efficiency was lower than ours, so the boss couldn't send all the orders to Huizhou. After the strike was over, the managers asked dozens of us to return to the factory. They even got some of the mechanics who had taken their compensation and left to rejoin the factory for a wage of thirty-two thousand yuan per month, with food and lodging included. They made everybody work themselves to death to make up the losses accrued during the strike.

Personally, I'm pretty direct. I can't read. My daughter is

in her third year of university. She studies art in Wuhan. The
tuition is seven thousand yuan, and I just gave her eleven thousand yuan. My parents are seventy years old and I have a lot
of people to think of, otherwise I could have supported the
workers' delegates more actively. Now I'm focused on my own
problems. My wife was at the same factory, and she just found
a new job today. I'm trying to get a job at a hardware factory.
For five eight-hour days a week without overtime, my wage will
be sixteen thousand yuan per month. There's a lot of pressure
on me. I'm forty-six years old this year. I'm getting old, so I'm
using my younger brother's ID card to get a job at a factory.

Ms. Liao

"What's the point of being a good employee when the boss is not good-hearted?"

The Beginning of the Strike

I got a job at the factory in 2007. I began in the second floor extrusion department, but this year I was moved to a first floor injection molding machine. The factory was relocating machinery even before 2007. In the past, there were forty-three plastic-framing machines on the second floor, but they were all relocated in 2010. More than ten bronzing machines were also relocated. Throughout the time I worked there, they were moving machinery every year.

When they were distributing red envelopes in 2013, Boss Two told the workers that the entire factory would be relocated in the following year. The management always had trouble hiring people. They apparently posted some kind of notice, but I'm not too sure what it was. Someone said they weren't moving machinery, and then the management hired a lot of casual workers. We'd worked there so long—if the factory wanted to do something, the boss should have discussed it with us.

Before the strike, they moved injection-molding machines twice. One time they moved two machines and the other time they moved one. We thought the boss would make a statement to us, but he never said anything, he just moved the machines. All four floors were emptied.

On the morning of the strike, they disassembled three machines. I was running machine five on that day. At the morning meeting, the foreman told us we would disassemble the machine once we'd finished our items. When the supervisor told us to disassemble the machines, who were we to talk back?

No matter what factory, the supervisors are at the top.

We were unable to continue once the injection-molding machine was loaded onto the truck, so we went out and blocked the truck in. We refused to let it leave and asked the boss to give a statement. Then the people from the second and third floors came out as well. There were four hundred people at the factory, and almost everyone was there. The foremen stood in the office building and looked out at us. I was thinking, the people in charge definitely know all about what's going on.

Boss Two's secretary came out and asked us what we thought we were doing. We said we wanted the boss to make a statement. The secretary told us to release the truck first. Meanwhile, an office worker inside called the boss.

Later, they moved a desk out of the office building and asked workers to come forward and resign to get their pay immediately. There were some people who left at that point, but they were all casual workers. I didn't know the ones that left. In any case, some people left. I saw them come forward and sign their names. Those casual workers said it was the same no matter where you worked and left. We thought it was bizarre. We just wanted a statement, so why were they asking people to resign?

I don't completely remember the first day, but on the second day a police officer came. You didn't see him, but he was mad as hell. We demanded he apologize to us.

Boss Two's Tricks

The first time the Labor Bureau came, there were three people. They were wearing casual clothes, not uniforms, and they said they were from the Investigation Office of the Labor Bureau. They wouldn't show us their identification when we asked, so we didn't believe them and refused to let them to enter. When they said they would resolve the issue for us, we asked how. They said they would base it on the labor laws regarding average monthly wage given per year and the high-temperature subsidy. They said that high-temperature subsidies were mandatory when the temperature exceeded thirty-six degrees Celsius, but you didn't receive it when it wasn't that hot. Also, it was only for situations where the temperature couldn't be decreased. Running the injection-molding machine was definitely high-temperature work. Many people surrounded them to ask questions.

I also asked those people from the Labor Bureau whether the labor laws applied only to certain locations. One said they didn't, that they were the same nationwide. In any case, if you left this location, you had to pay compensation. That's what the Labor Bureau said.

The boss didn't come out the first day. The government people went to the office building to talk to the secretary or somebody, but they wouldn't clarify things for us. They just entered the office building and stayed a long time.

Those Labor Bureau people came back to the factory every day. The second day of the strike, a large group came. But throughout the entire strike, I never saw their work credentials.

Boss Two came on the second day. He said he didn't know anything about the machines being moved to a different location. We asked him, "You don't know where your own machines are being moved? We may be employees but we're still part of this factory." He said he didn't know where they were being moved to because they were still searching for a factory building. Wasn't he trying to pull a quick one on us? He said those words with his own mouth.

We questioned him (there were many of us and it was crowded, so our voices were loud): "Boss, what do you think we are, three-year old children?" The boss told us to stop but we felt he was trying to trick us, so we didn't listen to what he was saying. When he asked us what we wanted, we said, "If you're relocating, you have to pay us. You have to compensate us."

Boss Two replied by asking us to move with the factory. We said we wanted to be compensated first. Once we were compensated, those who wanted to go could go and those who didn't want to wouldn't. Boss Two went back inside the office building without answering us.

Selecting Delegates

The people from the Labor Bureau asked us to select delegates. We didn't choose them on the first day, or on the second day. We didn't have any delegates at all. How would there be any delegates? There probably wasn't a single person willing to step out and speak for all of us. The selections had to be discussed because we had to unify our opinions before we could select delegates. On the third day, Boss Two still refused to come out, and the Labor Bureau, subdistrict office, and Public Security Bureau all asked us to select delegates.

We were also a little worried about selecting delegates, because we had heard of incidents like this: There was a factory furniture company that closed down, and when the workers selected a delegate, the boss paid him off. He left and many people were unable to get their money. Even after working at it for more than ten years, they got nothing. Most of the people at the factory had started before 1999 and been there ever since, so it was widely known. There were lots of people from my hometown at that factory. In the end none of them got their money, and all they could do was ask the Labor Bureau for one month's wage. There's still a senior employee at our factory who sleeps at the factory gates and still hasn't gotten his money. How could we select delegates? How could we trust them? Who could guarantee that the boss wouldn't buy off the delegates?

Up until the fourth or fifth day they said, "We can't discuss things with all of you at once. You say something and I say something, but I have no idea what you're saying." The boss also said that he couldn't make out what we were saying.

Later, each shop floor selected someone who was good at speaking, until there was a delegate for every shop floor. It took three days to do this. The delegate from our shop floor was our foreman. At first he wasn't willing to accept the position; I didn't choose him, someone else did. I couldn't tell you any of those delegates' names, I just know that two of them were foremen.

A Few Details about the Strike

During the strike, we just sat inside the factory grounds all day until we had finished dinner in the evening—one group here, one group there.

Volunteers watched the factory at night. The departments all took turns sending people for the night watch. Each department staffed the watch for one evening. If people from other departments wanted to come, they could. If they didn't want to, they didn't have to. There were probably thirty people there each night. The delegates organized the night watches.

One night the guards were watching the factory. They asked us to go home, so we did. That one day we weren't watching the factory, there was a fire.

From start to finish the strike took too long. Once when we were speaking to the management, everyone complained that every day was the same. They said they never even knew what time it was. We knew the boss had bought off the local government. The government was standing with the rich, so we wanted to go to the municipal government offices to question them. We scolded the delegates into coming even though none of them really wanted to at first.

As for marching to the municipal government, you could say that people were calling for a march every day just to see if anyone would respond. If someone did, they would go. Those people who visited the factory did nothing to resolve the issue. And, anyway, we had nothing to eat. Normally, food was provided during our shifts, but there was no food when we stopped work.

I moved for work in 2004 because I wanted to send my child to college and because I had to support my family. My husband couldn't use either of his legs, so he couldn't work at all. I worked out here alone to send my child to school. Everything costs money. When we're striking for so long, what can we eat? That's how it was. Anyway, people said they wanted to go there (the municipal government) and everyone went with them. There was no discussion.

One day it rained hard. I stayed in the factory dormitory playing cards, so I didn't see the boss. That was the day the Big Boss came to the factory. We were waiting the whole day and the Big Boss didn't come until two o'clock in the afternoon. I played cards with a few other workers in the dormitory. They said the Big Boss had come, but I didn't know who the Big Boss was and didn't recognize him.

On the last day, I went to the factory to get my money (wages and compensation). When I came out of the office building, I saw some people surrounding a man who was standing there. Someone said it was the Big Boss. When I went over, I heard him apologizing to us. He said, "You workers are great. You're very diligent." I said, "What use is it if we're good workers?" I said that right to him. "It's the boss that needs to be good. You were not a good-hearted boss." That's what I said. Then a supervisor took the boss and said, "Let's go. Don't listen to her."

Negotiations

On the first day of negotiations, there must have been almost three hundred of us outside waiting.

I tell you, if I had known they were going to release the truck, I would never have let it happen. I would have slept in the factory gates. To do such an important thing like that, I would definitely demand the boss make a statement. We took turns watching the truck, and I didn't know they were going to release it. There were also other people who said they didn't know it was going to be released.

The day we went to the township government, the delegates came out and said that the boss was willing to compensate us but we first had to release the machines. I remember that when we were in front of the government, a female delegate said, "Let the two vehicles go first." Later, we just went home. I personally went back to my apartment. I was feeling unwell because I'd thrown out my back, so I came late the next day. The next morning when I came at nine o'clock, I didn't know they had already released the truck. I asked where the vehicles had gone, and they told me they had been released. I said, "You've ruined everything. Now the boss will never compensate us."

The delegates came out but didn't say how much the boss would compensate us. We were foolish and had no experience with this kind of thing. I couldn't tell you why there weren't more people opposing the release of the truck. I don't know. Thinking about it now, I feel it was very foolish. They told us to go home and we went home. In the end, none of what the boss said was true, and the Big Boss never showed up. They took the truck trailer and the boss had people come for the two cars. In fact, we never saw him again. It made us so angry that we wanted go to the gates of the government offices.

At the Labor Bureau, the boss asked a lawyer to do the negotiating. I didn't go in. Only the delegates went in to negotiate. I heard them say they spoke to the lawyer for a long time but couldn't reach an agreement. When they asked the lawyer to call the boss, he said on the phone that he didn't want the factory. He said to let the workers make a fuss over it if they wanted to. The lawyer asked the boss to hurry back because the workers were following him everywhere, even to the bathroom. He wasn't even free to wash his hands. Then the boss hung up the phone. The delegates said it was fine if the boss didn't want the factory, but he had to fax over a document testifying that he didn't want it. With a boss like that, we definitely had to raise the issue with the government because they had promised to resolve the situation. They were the ones who asked us to release the boss's truck.

The First Time We Were Seized

The negotiation at the Labor Bureau and the trip to the township government were on the same day. When no results came from the negotiations at the Labor Bureau, we split up. It was past five o'clock by the time we arrived at the township government. At that point they said they were taking all of us to the police station.

None of the delegates asked us to march to the government offices. After the negotiations, they came out and stood at the entrance to the building. We asked them what had been discussed and they described the negotiations from start to finish. We said, "That's no good, no good at all. The government made promises to us, so we should go to the government." A group of us did go. At first everyone wanted to come along, but I said, "What help would it be to have all of you come? Watch over things here and don't let the lawyer leave." Everybody discussed it like that and then half of the people left for the government offices. The delegates didn't go with us to the government offices. Instead they all stayed at the Labor Bureau.

That's how it went. Some people watched over the lawyer and the management's representatives while others went to the township government.

When we got to the government office, we sat at the entrance and demanded the government make a statement. We sat there for half an hour and were seized sometime after six o'clock in the evening. I saw a great deal of Special Police gathering, their entire bodies covered in black. Some of us were loaded onto buses. They each held one arm and carried the people who wouldn't move. If you didn't let them carry yo,u they would grab you by the arms and legs. I said, "Let me go. I don't want to be seized. What law am I breaking? Where do you want me to go?" Some people struggled so the police used their elbows to beat them. That's how we were loaded into the buses. There was a woman who fainted and was hospitalized for three days. I didn't know her.

We were all taken to the Public Security Bureau. Inside,

we shouted and hollered. When the chief of the Public Security Bureau asked, "What are you shouting about?" I said, "We're hungry. We want something to eat and drink. We haven't had anything to eat for days." He gave us one bottle of water per person and later on we ate.

At nine o'clock the chief of police announced that we would be released, but we refused to go. It was after eleven and we wanted to eat at the Public Security Bureau. He promised that at nine the next morning he would help us sort it out and asked us to go home. He said he also needed to sleep, and that he couldn't help us figure things out if he didn't. We said, "You brought us here with buses, now you need to guarantee our safety and give us a ride back." That's right, we only went back when the government had made promises. If they come and take us in with buses, then they definitely should have dropped us off with the buses. But they weren't willing to, so we went home on our own.

At the Labor Bureau they held the lawyer and those people, but in the end, at around eight o'clock, they had no choice but to let them go. The next day we couldn't even find the lawyer.

Mr. Wu and one other delegate came to meet us at the police station. At that point we had been seized and everyone had eaten. They knew we'd been detained and they'd come by to check on us because they were worried. Mr. Wu said, "Everyone go home. Don't make a scene. Just do what they say." The workers' delegates told us to be obedient. They told us not to make it hard for the Special Police. Mr. Wu said, "The police have no say in the matter either. They'll help us take care of it tomorrow. Why don't we all just go home and rest?" Even though it was our delegates who urged us to go home, we still weren't willing to go. That was the situation. But ultimately, he was our delegate. We trusted him from the start and we selected him, so at that point we had to trust him again. Still, we didn't trust the government because they had already lied to us many times.

If they had had even one ounce of good faith the next

morning, we never would have gotten so angry. They said they would come at nine in the morning, but they were nowhere to be found. At eleven o'clock, they still didn't show. It wasn't until two o'clock that someone arrived. You can't trust the government at all. We were even angrier then.

People from the government, the Labor Bureau, and the Public Security Bureau all came together at two o'clock, but I couldn't say which was which.

That's how it went. The government came every day. They came every day, but the boss never showed his face. They said they would resolve the issue for us, but there wasn't a single day they really worked on it. They would come and just sit in the office building. Sometimes they asked to speak to the delegates for a while.

Regarding the Road Blockage

We never blocked the road. We just took a banner and marched from here to there and back. Actually, come to think of it, we did block the road in front of the gate the first time. That time I didn't take part because of my back. I was worried something horrible would happen to my back if I fell down or was hit. I participated in a lot of things, but that time I just watched from afar. A bunch of cops came out to force us back to the factory. I didn't know that in the struggle someone fell and broke their arm. The police took her to the hospital.

The boss appeared the next day. He asked us not to obstruct the road and promised to resolve the issue. We believed him again and again we let them go. The road blockage was no one's idea. Everyone was just spending every day there discussing how bad things were.

I had seen one road blockage before. It was at an electronics plant where the boss had relocated and refused to pay. Those people blocked the road until the cars were backed up to Wanlian Mall, and half an hour later, the boss gave them the money. We all saw it happen.

Mr. Wu and the other delegates didn't come out when we blocked the road, nor did the foremen. The road was so narrow that just ten people standing in the middle was enough to stop traffic from getting through.

After the first time we blocked the road at the factory gates, we marched in a big circle. There were three Special Police and two government officials that went with us. As we walked on and on, I said to the police officer, "My back hurts too much to go on." He was on a motorbike, so I asked him to let me ride. He said, "If I let you ride, I'll be breaking the law. Who told you to march?" I said, "If you had taken care of the situation earlier, none of us would be out here marching." Later, I even made a joke with the officer. I said, "We're walking here and we even have you as bodyguards." That officer had to smile.

The delegates also asked our opinions. We wanted the boss to compensate us. After all, the Labor Bureau told us how much we should be compensated. The amount was set by the law. That was as much as we understood. None of us understood the law, and some were illiterate. How would we know about such things? We just knew money. That's how it was. Many people said we would block the road if they didn't compensate us. We didn't understand the law, but if we saw someone taking action, we followed their example.

The Second Time We Were Seized

The day we went to petition at the municipal government offices, I had just arrived at the factory's gates when I saw people coming out. I followed them because I knew they were going on another march. We walked for a time and saw that there were people following us. Mr. Wu asked us to wait two more days because the government said they would address the issue. But who was still listening to him? People said, "The strike hasn't been just one or two days. We've been waiting here every day. What are we waiting for? If we want to petition the municipal government, let's go do it." We still didn't know which way the offices were and we couldn't figure it out. I didn't know any of the people who were leading us in the front. The people from the Labor Bureau and Public Security Bureau kept following us. They didn't stop us, but I wasn't sure why.

It seems there were around six government and security personnel who left with us from the factory gates. The police told us to go back but we refused. We said, "We'll go back if you can resolve this problem for us. If you can't, then we're going to petition the municipal government." They were unable to stop us. They said, "No matter what your reason is, you cannot block the roads." We said, "We aren't blocking the road. We're just walking along it. If someone would resolve the problem, we would go back. But if you can't resolve it, then there's no point in discussing it." When we had just started, we weren't blocking the entire road. As we walked farther, we spread out and then we were blocking the road.

We were at a three-way intersection, I'm not sure of its exact location, when the cops arrived. They wanted to block the people in the front and stop us from going on. Many of us cursed them. Everyone wanted to speak to them at once. We said, "We're going to petition the government. What are you doing blocking the road? Can you resolve the problem for us?" That's what we said. The officers didn't reply but then they let us through and just continued to follow us. Someone in the front was photographing us. They took photos of us the whole way. As soon as we left the gates, there was someone photographing us.

We walked and walked. I don't know where we walked to, but suddenly more police came out and seized all of us. There were a lot of police, more than I could count. There were a lot of us and a lot of police. The police were beating people.

The officers told us to stop walking and stand by the side of the road. They said if we stood to one side, they would come address the issue. We weren't willing to stand to one side, so they beat us with their fists, with their elbows, and with their feet. My buddy's (*ge*) flip-flop had fallen off, and when he tried to pick it up, they beat him until his back hurt.

All of us were sobbing. I began crying and cursing them at the same time. I said, "You were born to mothers! If your mother was working somewhere and ran into this situation, what would you do?" I said it again and again and again. A few of the police officers cried together with us. It was the officers who had walked with us from the factory. I said, "It's hard for us who moved here to find work (*dagong*). We're not out here striking for just one or two days. What is it you think we want? We just want to go to petition the government, and you're here beating and kicking us."

Later, they brought a big bus and told us to get in. I said "I'll get in the bus if you want me to, but I haven't committed any crime. We're just demanding that the issue be resolved." I was the first in the bus. One bus could fit dozens of us. There was a police officer standing next to each seat.

No one but Mr. Wu was handcuffed. On the bus, we saw him with officers on either side of him holding his arms. He had handcuffs on. We shouted from the truck. We asked what law he broke and why they needed to handcuff him. Mr. Wu said there was no problem. He told us not to worry about him.

I realized they weren't taking us to the municipal government. They turned around and they began driving us back. We started cursing them on the bus and scolded them for a while. I called a worker from my hometown and asked where he was. He said he was in a different bus.

We were seized at two o'clock in the afternoon and released twenty-four hours later. After questioning us, they asked us to sign a printed document. They wanted photographs and confessions. They asked me if I had cursed the police and I said I had. I replied, "Who are the people's police there for? For the people. So now this officer, was he there for the people or for our boss? I say you're there for the boss." I asked him that. When he asked me who the delegates were, I said, "You're asking me who the delegates are? You're the ones who made us pick them. We don't have delegates. If you hadn't made us choose them, we never would have had them. How can we trust someone to speak for us? No one can speak for another person." They also asked about the fire. I said, "Your people were in there that night, not ours. How would we know what happened?"

Then they gave me the transcript of the questioning. He had written down everything I said. He didn't say he wouldn't let me read it. Then he had me look at photos and asked who the delegates were. I said I didn't know. Whenever he asked me I just said I didn't know. Later, an officer got angry with me. I said, "If your mother got into a situation like this, I'd see whether you got upset or not." He had no reply. The officer said, "You seem pretty honest, so we'll let you go."

After Release

I didn't go to the factory on the day I was released. Instead, I went to bed. I'm not sure which day it was that I went back to the factory. They returned my cell phone when they released me.

The day after we were released, some people went to sit in front of the factory again because we still hadn't gotten our money. Others were held for more than ten days before being released.

After we got out, many of us were scared. The secretary told us that those who didn't want to work were resigning but those who wanted to work could sign their names and resume work. Some people left. Some people never got a single penny in compensation; they left with only their back wages. More than ten people left without being compensated. There were also people who signed and went back to work. After being held in the Public Security Bureau for one night, many people were scared. Many people just took their wages and left.

After my release, I found a place offering casual employment. One day I was working there when my old coworker called and asked why I hadn't come. He said everyone had gotten their money and left. I was the only one who hadn't signed. I asked him to sign for me and he did. I hurried over later. It was after six o'clock that afternoon by the time I got my wages.

Some people who were released went to the Public Security Bureau to check on the people who hadn't been released, but many people weren't willing to go with them. The Public Security Bureau wouldn't even let them in the door, so they just went home. I went back to my hometown and returned one month later.

About Myself

My hometown is Guangxi. I lived my whole life there until 2004. When my child started middle school, I came to Shenzhen to find work and found a position at a factory. In 2007, the factory moved to a five-day workweek (*shuangxiu*). I had three children in school, and with two days off per week I couldn't afford to keep them all in school. My sister used to work at a market here selling pork. Now my kids have finished college, but they still haven't found work.

My children are grown now but no one in the family has bought an apartment. They still haven't finished paying back the money they borrowed for college, so we carry a great deal of burdens. My husband was bitten by a snake in 2006. His treatment cost almost four thousand yuan. Just six months after his recovery, he was paralyzed. He couldn't even use chopsticks, and the treatment took another six months. It cost more than a hundred yuan per day, so we spent all of the money we had saved to buy an apartment. Half a year after his treatment ended, he was able to walk and eat on his own again, but then he died just six months later. Before all of that, my husband was a capable man. We relied on him alone to earn money and I stayed at home taking care of the family. Once he died my mother-in-law lost her mind for three years. My husband never went back to work and later he got rheumatism.

After leaving the factory where the strike happened, I started at a different factory with a slightly higher wage. Before I had to work twelve hours a day, now I work just eleven. The basic monthly wage is sixteen hundred yuan. We generally get twelve yuan per hour for overtime but on Saturday and Sunday we get fifteen. We have a hundred-yuan-per-month housing allowance and one hundred fifty yuan per month for living expenses. The perfect attendance award is fifty yuan. Together with the base wage, it's nineteen hundred yuan per month. The factory is new. It's pretty small, just a dozen people in total. There are three bosses, all of them from northern China. We make hardware. We have Sundays off and an eight-hour workday on Saturday. There's no Social Insurance of any type. They pay us on the 28th of each month.

Ms. Tian

"We had come out twice before, so we assumed this time would be no different."

In August 2010, I began working at the factory for the second time. I had worked there once before but later transferred to a different factory. Compared to nearby factories, which were largely unstandardized, this factory was relatively standardized. Although we didn't get double wages on Saturday, they usually paid the overtime rates required by the labor laws. We generally worked four hours overtime per day and they paid our wages on the 22nd of each month. One portion of it was transferred to your bank account, and a few days later they would distribute the rest in cash. While we were still on strike (the beginning of the month), the boss just put all of the money in our accounts. As to why they paid the wages so early, I would guess it was because the government came to investigate and the boss said that wages were always distributed during the first week of the month. After the strike, the boss put the money in the workers' accounts early each month so they wouldn't have to make excuses if the government put pressure on them.

In regard to the delegate who began this strike, Mr. Wu, the boss had long been dissatisfied with him. Over the past several years, the government came periodically to inspect the factory. Before they came, the management would teach everyone how to respond. If they surveyed you and you lied, the management gave you two hundred yuan. We had two wage slips: one slip was our actual wage slip for distributing wages and the other was to show the people who inspected the factory. They deducted three hundred yuan from our pay each month for food. It was deducted no matter whether you ate or not, and you couldn't take the food to go. The food in the cafeteria was terrible, so why not let us take it to go and make something at home? But the management wouldn't allow it. One time they questioned Mr. Wu while they were inspecting the factory and he told the truth. I don't know whether or not the government fined the boss, but they stopped deducting the dining fee after that, and only those who ate paid it.

This incident made the boss angry, so he cut Mr. Wu's overtime. Later, when the boss was still hiring child workers, Mr. Wu complained to the labor station. The boss must have thought that the stalemate wasn't working, because he let Mr. Wu work overtime again.

When the boss was holding the year-end prize drawing (*choujiang*), he said the whole factory would move to Huizhou and that he wanted everyone to come with him. As a result, some people resigned and left. Of the more than one thousand original employees, there were only four hundred left. Though there were plenty of orders, they were all being sent to Huizhou and there was no overtime. That year, the boss had already relocated machinery twice. The third time, he used a flatbed truck. When the truck was loaded, we started the strike and demanded economic compensation. A foreman from the fourth floor work team organized the workers to obstruct the truck. People from the first floor went out first and those from the third and fourth floors followed behind. When the boss's secretary came out of the building, she said the injection-molding goods needed to be sent out from the Huizhou factory, so they needed to relocate the machinery. She asked everyone to step back and stop blocking the truck, but we didn't listen. That day two or three workers went to the Labor Bureau to file a complaint. The Labor Bureau said to first ask the township labor station to resolve the problem. Someone from the township labor station came, but I couldn't make out what they were saying. They asked us to select delegates.

We took shifts watching the factory and refused to let the boss take any of the machines. But we stopped guarding the factory when the Labor Bureau personnel promised us they would stop the boss from moving the machinery. Coincidentally, during the two days when workers weren't guarding it, a corrugated iron building in the factory caught on fire. The media came to interview people because of the fire, but they weren't interested in the workers' problems with compensation. The boss didn't show up, either. Discussing it later, we agreed that even a big fire couldn't burn the boss.

We discussed the amount of compensation during the negotiations. Though we did not understand the law, we knew how other factories were compensating workers. But our boss was not a kind-hearted boss. He refused to compensate us, and he even said he would spend ten million yuan to break the strike.

During the strike, people from the Labor Bureau said, "Your boss is a lazy dog. He doesn't come out to negotiate, and we can't do anything about it. If he was holding your wages, we could speak to him, but he's not, and there's no such thing as compensation for leaving the factory." No one was happy to hear that. We all wanted to go to the municipal Labor Bureau to seek an audience, but we had to walk because we had no money to take a bus. Mr. Wu was unlucky. He didn't want to go to the government offices. At first, he was waiting in the factory, but he decided that if everyone was determined to go, he wouldn't be able to look us in the face if he didn't. So, he came along.

When we sought an audience, there were police officers following us the whole way and taking photos. If the group blocked the road, the officers would ask us to make a path. If we refused, they forced their way through. The cars on the road didn't come at us honking their horns. Some of the drivers stopped and took video of the commotion until the police officers stopped them. Halfway there the police started to seize people. Some workers ran to hide in the toilets. They seized around 180 people and detained us in five nearby police stations. I was held for twenty-four hours. I was given only one bottle of water and one piece of bread, and I had to sleep on the floor. The police recorded my confession and asked who had encouraged people to take to the streets. I said, "No one encouraged us. We just wanted to go." They released me the next day. Ten other workers were held for ten days and two were held for a month, but Mr. Wu continued to be detained and still has not been released.

We now regret going out onto the road that day. We really shouldn't have; we hurt Mr. Wu. But we had gone out twice before. One time we left from the factory gates and blocked the road for several minutes, and the other time we marched in a big loop carrying a banner. No one cared then, so we thought no one would care the next time. I don't know why they seized people that day.

After we were released from the police station, the management hung a notice that said employees who didn't want to work would receive compensation from the management of four hundred yuan per year worked. They also agreed to give us holiday pay for the past two years. Those who wanted to continue to work could do so, but the management fired twenty-four people and hung a list of their names. Everyone was equally compensated, but there was no pay for the time we were on strike. We thought, "The factory is relocating anyway. Now at least we can get some compensation. Later, who can say if we'll get anything at all?" So, we took the money and left the factory. Some people went back to work there. When the ten people who were being held were released, they got the same compensation.

Several Women Workers Have Their Say

"Just as I was about to go, an officer kicked me."

After the first day of the strike, we visited to the Labor Bureau. The people there said that if the issue couldn't be resolved, we could just do whatever we wanted (meaning we could raise any kind of ruckus). It was the Labor Bureau personnel who told us we could block the road. But when we actually went to block the road, the government seized people. Now they still haven't been released.

I didn't know Mr. Wu at first, but after the strike everyone spent a lot of time chatting and we got to know one another. When Mr. Wu let them take those machines from the factory, we let him have it. He was not acting on our behalf when he did that.

After we'd gone on strike, we spoke to the employees of other factories, saying that we were from the factory that was striking, and we were fighting for compensation. They told us, "You'll never win over your boss. In the past, he was the kind who would come out and fight." We heard there was a previous strike at the factory that the boss broke.

When we began the strike, the boss told us they weren't going to move the factory, but we didn't believe it. We said, "First pay all of our back wages so whoever wants to work can keep working and whoever wants to go can go." But the boss refused. With so many of the machines already moved, what could we do?

The management's lawyer came, and we wouldn't let him leave. We demanded at least one month's wages, sixteen thousand yuan, in compensation. The lawyer said he had no authority and told us to ask the boss. But if you can't make decisions, why are you here? We only let the lawyer go when someone from the labor station gave us a written guarantee that the boss would meet us.

On the last day of the strike, at the entrance to the highway, Special Police surrounded us petitioners. When I saw the Special Police beating people from my hometown, I went to ask them why they were attacking us. Just as I was about to go, an officer kicked me.

When they were taking confessions, the cops would point at photos and ask if you knew this person or that person. Then they took fingerprints. It was heavy-handed.

Appendix: Relocation Struggle at a Uniqlo Supplier, 2014 to 2015

This clothing factory was opened with Hong Kong capital at the end of the 1980s. Although it initially had only a few dozen workers, the factory was constantly expanding, and around 2005, the total number of workers had reached roughly three thousand.

After 2008, the factory gradually began to outsource (*waifa*) orders, reduce production, and decrease the number of employees. In 2011, the factory stopped hiring, and by the first strike in December 2014, there were only eight hundred workers left. The majority of them were women, and many had been there over a decade—some more than two decades.

There had never been an all-factory strike at the factory, and most workers had no experience with collective struggle before they took action. Their two strikes, with a truce (*xiuzhanqi*) in the intervening period, lasted a total of eight months. The first strike was brief, lasting from December 10 to December 18, 2014. Their main demand was compensation for unpaid pensions and housing funds. The second strike was longer, lasting from June 9 to July 15, 2015, and was for economic compensation.

Part One: The December Strike

Workers initiated the December strike. Activist workers (*gon-gren jijifenzi*) performed the most basic organizational work by distributing materials and agitating before the strike was called. As for the factory management, although shop-floor supervisors discovered workers were signing a joint letter, the management level seems to have made no preparations for how to respond to the strike.

At the start of the strike, the workers locked up the factory, putting pressure on the employer and causing losses. Besides stopping the employer from shipping goods and sending delegates to petition relevant government departments, the workers did not take any other direct actions to put pressure on the employer and government during the stalemate (for example, causing road blockages).

While the factory was locked down, there was, in fact, no development in the workers' organizing. During discussions of action strategies and analyses of the situation, the participation rate among common workers was low. With the cooperation of the government, the employer was communicating with the workers. But at the same time, they were coordinating their power internally and externally and making a careful plan to strike back. On the morning of the ninth day, the boss personally brought a great number of riot police to force the workers back to the shop floor. Then the employer used a series of measures to force and coerce the workers to resume normal production.

Below is a brief summary of what happened during the December strike.

How Did the Strike Begin?

A female worker described the strike as an "uprising" (*baodong*) or a "riot" (*dabaoluan*). Although this may be a bit exaggerated, it reflects the fact that the workers were immersed in an atmosphere of rebellion.

The workers' high morale was driven not only by the goals

of their struggle but also by the anxiety and dissatisfaction that had been accumulating long before the strike was called. The anxiety was caused by worries that the factory would relocate; the dissatisfaction because incomes had decreased.

Word that the factory would relocate spread among the workers as early as 2008. The government acquired land for subway construction in 2014, and though it was clearly visible that they were demolishing nearby factories, the employer continued to insist that they were not relocating. As a result, workers began to worry they would not be compensated when the factory relocated. In addition, workers had been getting fewer overtime hours for the past several years and were unhappy with the decreases this caused in their incomes. Some workers who had no overtime at all were earning only fourteen thousand to fifteen thousand yuan per month after Social Insurance payments. With the normal production atmosphere of the factory in decline, people panicked and complaints broke out on all fronts. In this regard, the psychological conditions were ripe for widespread participation in the strike.

If, under these circumstances, the workers had been able to put forward goals everyone could agree upon and summarize them into demands that were plausible, reasonable, and legal, they may have been able to transform that widespread unhappiness and dissatisfaction into collective action.

The collective demands of the December strike were organized with the assistance of a labor NGO. The organization had previously distributed pamphlets on labor law near the factory. One day, in October 2014, a female worker who was worried they wouldn't be compensated when the factory relocated called the organization and consulted with an employee there. The employee asked her to gather a few other workers for a face-to-face meeting. It was only through these discussions that the workers learned there were many legal violations in the factory. Still, the timing was not yet right to demand economic compensation, because the employer was still denying that the factory was relocating. The workers accepted the recommendation of the organization: focus on the infringements on legal rights and benefits such as pensions and the housing funds. They would first return to the factory and spread materials, then organize the workers to put forward collective demands and carry out collective actions in defense of their rights.

This is how, with the assistance of an organization, a small resistance group was organized from a few activist workers. They began spreading materials to other workers, writing a joint letter, and collecting worker signatures. By the start of December, they had 710 signatures on their letter and had received twenty yuan from each person to create a rights advocacy fund.

On December 1, the workers registered a microblog account and began sending out messages about the fight for their rights.

On December 5, the workers submitted their joint letter to the employer and asked for a response by December 8. We learn from their microblog posts that if the factory employer did not provide a satisfactory answer during the allotted time, the workers planned to complain at the Housing Fund Management Center and the labor investigations department.

On December 9, the employer announced they would investigate the microblog.

Having received no response from the employer, the activist workers decided to collectively ask for a statement from the employer. People were generally not interested in working, and when they saw some people leaving their stations, they all left the production lines together.

The organization's employees did not know the workers were going to strike; the workers' delegates only informed them of it after the fact. Many workers were also initially unaware of the strike, but the activist workers said they were conscious of a collective decision to initiate it. They were successful.

The Stalemate Period of the Strike

There was an eight-day stalemate before the workers were cleared by force on December 18. Despite constant friction between labor and capital, no major conflicts broke out.

During the first days of the strike, worker morale was high. Intuiting that conditions were not good, the boss did not show his face during this time. Only a few high-level managers met with the workers to make verbal promises and delay.

During this period, the employer was constantly making small moves. After two attempts to ship goods on December 11 failed, they posted the factory rules and regulations in a prominent location and tried to force the workers to respect the regulations. On the 13th, they cut water and power to the worker dormitories. On the 15th, the management made a promise: "The company will give employees who come to work on time and stay busy an additional twenty yuan per day in compensation. Those who miss work without reason will be considered absent." The workers immediately looked with disdain on this statement by the employer, saying, "Hey, this is a strike!"

Among strikes like this in recent years, it has become rare for bosses and high-level management to use the method of "coaxing"—treating the workers like small children and immediately giving them benefits in order to appease their emotions and have them resume work as soon as possible—to deal with the workers. The employers immediately resort to the authority of normal factory production: that is, to the factory's regulations. Coercing and luring have become the standard methods of dealing with strikes.

When the management's authority is suddenly voided, such posturing only seems comical to the workers. The company had to pay tremendous fines to clients because they were unable to ship goods, but the boss was unwilling to negotiate "under duress." As such, he had his hands tied in regard to the workers who "rebelled," before he "brought in troops" (*daibing*) to clear them out.

Before the government "loaned its troops" (*jiebing*) to the boss, their attitude toward him was neither warm nor cool. The government workers who rushed to the factory were business-like. They were noncommittal regarding the action taken by workers to lock the factory, and when the workers demanded compensation for unpaid pensions, they replied, for the ump-teenth time, with the well-known phrase, "It takes two years to effectively prosecute such a case."

On December 15, the employer posted a notice in the fac-tory saying the management had "decided that elections would be held for selecting employee delegates. . . . Every department shall use democratic elections with the assistance of the em-ployee care center." As one worker explained,

> The employers gave us a paper and asked us to vote, but we didn't dare vote. The paper was blank. It had no candidate names on it. They just asked us to write people in. We didn't dare. Everyone said as soon as we write something down, those people will be seized. Later, someone was clever and said we would all write down the supervisors and foremen. When we did, those votes weren't counted. The management got out a blackboard and wrote the candidates' names directly.
>
> No one told us the delegates would be seized, but that was our concern. Only a few people wrote on the slips of paper. When they gave them to us, we didn't accept them. At that time we just wanted to have a discussion. It would be best to discuss things with the boss. That's what everyone thought. We were also worried about what would happen if the delegates were bought out. If he ignored us, what would we do? That was another concern.

Though the workers initially resisted the management's del-egate elections, everyone knew who the leaders were. They were the activists who had laid the foundation for the strike. Those women had also become true organizers once the strike was called. Ultimately, those were the people who were elected as delegates for the so-called "consultations" with the management. According to another worker's testimony,

> We didn't hold an all-factory meeting because we couldn't hold such a meeting. Sometimes someone would accidentally let something slip. We were worried about the risks, worried someone would be seized. It was the delegates who agreed everything, and in the evenings the liaisons would notify all the shifts. Generally, they only made announcements in the evenings.
>
> During last year's strike, I slept directly on the concrete hallway outside of the shop floor. . . . The shop floor leader didn't take part. When the shift was ending, we locked the shop floor. During the day I played cards with a big group of people. Everyone slept at night.

Although striking was difficult, most of the employees had almost nothing to do besides play cards and sleep. All they did was listen to the delegates' decisions announced by the liaisons, either by phone or in person. From a strike-organizing standpoint, the participation level among common workers was quite low. Information flowed mostly in one direction and the analysis and judgment of the situation was basically limited to the labor NGO and the small circle of delegates.

The workers had no experience striking, so they didn't know what to think or what to do. A portion of the active participants felt unqualified to act, so they thought it would be enough to leave the meetings, assignments, and negotiations to those who could speak eloquently or had some understanding of the law. There were also a great number of workers who had, to some extent, a hitchhiking mentality. They hid in the back and let "those people" jump out in front, knowing the benefits they fought for would naturally accrue to them as well. This caused a great deal of resentment among some active workers, who said, "Everyone was hiding in the back. Sometimes not a single person was willing to step forward."

As the workers' enthusiasm waned, the boss was preparing an attack on the strike.

Clearing the Area, Conducting Sabotage, and Resuming Work

On the afternoon of December 17, the employer posted a notice that they would negotiate with the workers at ten o'clock the next morning.

That evening, some workers learned from hometown friends in the security services that the police would be seizing people the next day. The workers' delegates and the NGO staff had a simple discussion of this but did not notify the other workers. Everyone thought that since the boss had already agreed to negotiate, seizures were unlikely.

At eight o'clock the next morning, the boss appeared at the factory gates surrounded by a great number of cops. One worker recounted,

> When the boss came on the 18th, we still thought it was good news. Who knew a bunch of thugs (*lanzi*) would come? . . . He said, "You need to struggle for the company." After saying a few sentences, he asked us to go to work. He didn't respond to any of the demands we raised.
>
> At seven o'clock the personnel and supervisors—basically everyone from the high level management—showed up. Around 7:30, a lot of cops came. The place was filled with cops, at least a thousand.. . . It was horrifying. I was so scared my legs went weak.

With the protection of layers upon layers of "thugs," the boss didn't even finish the nonsense he was spouting. Some workers took out their wage slips and stepped forward to discuss them, but before they'd said more than a few sentences, the police began to seize people.

One woman said she'd never seen so many police in her life. Although they feel angry when thinking back on it, at the

time no one had experienced anything like it. Being psycho-
logically unprepared, many workers became frightened.

There were some scuffles when people were being seized,
but nothing serious. Everything went as planned: the workers
were forced back to the shop floor and the delegates were seized
with some other troublesome (*bulaoshi*) workers and taken to
the police station. Of course, the workers had not organized
any resistance.

The government's deterrent of "sending in troops" impec-
cably completed the work of the "big stick" and helped the boss
retake control of the factory. Able to seamlessly ship orders, the
boss breathed a sigh of relief.

After the government had "withdrawn the troops," they
arranged for a number of police officers and security personnel
to be stationed in the shop floor. They both patrolled and used
video equipment to record and monitor the work being done.
This maintained a certain level of pressure.

Though the workers who were forced back to the shop floor
were scared, they were suppressing their fury and did not com-
pliantly return to work. Instead, they quietly began to carry out
sabotage.

At this point, the employer quickly pulled out a carrot in
order to get the workers to resume normal production: a one-
day offer of one hundred yuan for anyone who resumed work
that morning and fifty yuan for anyone who resumed work that
afternoon:

> Those people had come back and, seeing how powerful the
> others were, they felt helpless and scared. But they could
> still get a hundred yuan. One-third of the group went back
> to work that morning.[19]

In those high-pressure circumstances, workers were lured
into resuming work. This was the second consecutive attack on
the strike. The workers were divided, and the boss was victori-
ous once again.

To solidify the results and further wipe out any resistance among the workers, the employer made a verbal promise to raise the minimum wage from 2,030 yuan to 2,500 yuan (this was never fulfilled). They also adjusted the orders so the workers would have sufficient overtime before the New Year. With the New Year holiday almost upon them, the workers were getting overtime and earning money. More and more workers resumed work. "They returned to putting their all in it."

As for the main demand that unpaid Social Insurance be reimbursed, the employers were clearly acting illegally. Because the workers had already filed a complaint about the situation, the government had no legal reason to refuse it, and the employers acquiesced and "generously" agreed to the demand. Though the workers were deeply dissatisfied with the proposal for distributing the six years of back benefits, it was forced upon them and they had no choice but to accept.

In the days after the workers were cleared out, the All-China Federation of Trade Unions (ACFTU) came forward to facilitate "consultations" between the management and the workers' delegates, but these so-called consultations were just unilateral announcements on the part of the employers as to how they would address the situation.

Although significant power had been exercised, there remained some employees who refused, from start to finish, to sign the agreement for distributing the six years of owed benefits. Regardless of whether the workers signed or not, the employer compensated the funds for all employees.

Several workers and activists couldn't swallow this. In January, they returned to the municipal Housing Fund Management Center to complain and petitioned the provincial ACFTU, but there were no results.

The workers who were arrested when people were cleared out on December 18 were quickly released. The employer also did not fire any workers. But some activists were assigned to do their work in a small room. They were separated from the other workers and not given overtime. There was also a camera installed in the room they worked in.

The December strike had concluded, but some remnants remained. First, the issues with the pensions still had not been resolved. Second, it led to the June strike in the following year, in response to factory relocation. Although the demands of this strike did not touch on relocation compensation, the workers' delegates brought the issue up during the "consultations" after work had resumed. All they got was a verbal promise that there would be a one-month warning before the factory was relocated.

"Peace" had been restored, but it lasted only five months.

Part Two: The June Strike

When work began in 2015, overtime continued to gradually decrease. By April, there were only five eight-hour days per week. During this period, the employers continued to harass the active workers' delegates from the December strike. They did not give them overtime and tried to make them leave. Several female workers made a fuss in the factory and stopped the employer from succeeding.

Just before May, the employers finally began acting on their plan to relocate the factory. A notice was posted on April 30, informing workers that the cutting bed department would be moved. The notice naturally did not say the factory would be relocated, nor did it mention the issue of economic compensation. The warehouse department was also moved in May. Most of the workers affected by these two relocations were men:

> They moved the cutting bed and warehouse departments before June 9. During the December strike, those men gave it their all and made quite a lot of noise. When the second floor didn't come down, they went up and shouted, "Everyone come down." . . . The management used money to tempt them, and was already offering more than three thousand yuan per person. Because we only had the basic wage here

(in the old factory) and no overtime, we were only making twelve hundred yuan per month. The male workers thought of that sum, more than three thousand yuan, and signed the contract. . . . With those two departments gone, there were only a dozen or so men remaining. We were all scared senseless and couldn't act out. When people are seized, they seize men first, so they were afraid to take action.

But no one went out to stop it. We were from the shop floor, and no one dared go out and obstruct it. If we were going to act, we probably should have stopped them from taking the cutting beds. But because they were only moving the men's machines, it didn't prevent us from working. That's what we thought at the time. . . . We were scared because of what happened last year, so no one dared obstruct them.[20]

The female workers did not take action to stop the employers from relocating the cutting bed and warehouse departments. Later, one delegate would say she had recommended going out to block the management from moving the departments but received no response from the other delegates. The matter just went unresolved. As a side note, the cutting bed is a relatively large machine that the management considers to be profitable equipment.

Between March and May, the workers' delegates from the December strike took part in some activities organized by the NGO. Some were summaries, discussions, and presentations about fighting for workers' rights, while others were social. The NGO wanted to maintain contact with the activist workers, summarize the experiences from the December strike, and encourage them to continue organizing.

But in truth, they did nothing during this period. The general reasons were as follows: First, they were frustrated after the December strike failed. Second, they were under a great deal of pressure and weren't willing to stick their necks out. Third, the disappearance and selfishness of other workers had left them disillusioned. Fourth, they had no experience; they wanted to intervene but weren't sure where to begin. To sum up the conclusions of the discussions they participated in, they "needed to strengthen their organizing work." To this, they could only laugh.

The activists needed to take on the tasks of inciting and organizing a strike. They were facing tremendous pressure from the employers and government. Without other workers organizing to ensure and support their efforts, the pressure was enough to leave them feeling paralyzed.

In terms of the disappearance or selfishness of other workers, the dissatisfaction of many who initially participated in the collective action had been mollified by the work resumption bonus and the adequate overtime. The activists may not have fully recognized this point from the beginning: because they couldn't get into a rhythm of collective action, they were overwhelmed by all sorts of negative feelings and a gap formed between them in the workers' collective.

The activists could only wait on the enthusiasm of the other workers before they could serve a purpose because they were unable to affect either the emotions of many workers or the incidents that would trigger collective action.

When the warehouse and cutting bed departments had been moved without difficulty, the workers were unable to sit by any longer. The delegates sought assistance from the NGO again. As a result of their discussions, they decided to again put forward a call for collective bargaining and ask that the employer respond within three days.

A Dismissal: The Boss Provokes the Strike

On June 2, the workers' delegates gave the employer the request for collective bargaining, and he ignored it:

> What would happen after giving the request to the management? That may be something the delegates needed to discuss internally. We didn't think of striking again. We

thought it would be that simple. (*Laughs* . . .)[21]

The three days passed quickly, and the workers took no action in response to the employer's refusal to answer. However, the management was preparing to provoke the strike.

There was one female factory worker, "Worker F," who was past retirement age. During those days, she was constantly calling on the management to deal with the issue of her owed pension. She did not ask that they deal exclusively with her problem, but that the employer compensate the pensions of all those who had reached retirement age. It was said that the management offered her one hundred fifty thousand yuan on the condition that she resign and stop participating in fights for her rights, but she refused. On the evening of June 8, Worker F received a text message saying that she had been dismissed. The management claimed it was due to her age and demanded that she go through the procedures of resigning the following day.

Worker F was an honest employee. She had not been an activist during the December strike and was not a delegate. There were many women over the age of fifty working at the factory, but she may have been axed because during the December strike the workers' delegates often met at her house—she rented a large apartment.

On the morning of the 9th, Worker F was stopped outside the factory by security when she tried to sign in. An argument immediately broke out. When a portion of the workers getting ready inside the shop floor heard what was happening, they gathered at the factory gates to support Worker F. The June strike had begun.

As more and more workers gathered at the factory gates, the management called the police. The police arrived on the scene and asked Worker F to come alone into the offices. When she refused, an officer stepped forward and seized her. He forcibly pulled her toward the office building. When Worker F fell to the ground, her fingers scraped the officer's arm. The officer immediately charged her with "disrupting public order" and "assaulting an officer." She was forced into a police car and taken to the police station.

From the 9th until the 11th, the workers gathered daily at the police station to demand Worker F's release. At one point, they had close to three hundred people surrounding the station. The police mobilized a large number of riot police to maintain order. More than a dozen people were seized and held for hours at a time. Taking advantage of the fact that the workers were not in the factory, the employer moved more machines and goods.

Besides surrounding the station, the workers repeatedly petitioned the subdistrict and district governments. They demanded that the government intervene and put pressure on the management, but the government did not take action.

Finding their tactics ineffective, the workers began "clocking in" on the 12th in order to avoid being deemed absent by the management. They watched over the factory and slept at night in the shop floor. At the same time, the workers began preparations to petition the municipal government.

On the 13th, around a hundred workers headed separately to the municipal government. When they gathered on-site, police quickly surrounded them. Under the urging of the police, the workers reluctantly boarded buses back to the factory. A small number of observant workers did not gather with the large group. They instead met with Bureau Chief Huang of the Municipal Petitions Office. Huang had compassion for the workers and told them their demands were reasonable and legal. He promised he would have the local government help the workers resolve the issue. Although the ball was still passed off to the local government, the workers were heartened by Bureau Chief Huang's attitude.

Some workers were uncertain what the "kind-hearted" Bureau Chief Huang had said, but the results of their petitioning did not surprise them. They said, "We've been caught again," and thought, "No one in the government is listening to us. No one cares."

From Tuesday (the 9th) when the strike began to Saturday (the 13th) when they petitioned the municipal government, the workers were forced to organize multiple collective actions both within the factory and beyond it. In just five days, a strike in the factory developed into surrounding the police station and marching to the subdistrict and district government offices. Ultimately, it led them to the last resort: petitioning the municipal government.

The employers were not idle during these days. Rather, they spent the whole time luring those workers who had not participated in the strike to begin working at the new factory:

> On June 9, there were still seven or eight hundred work-
> ers in the factory. By the 15th, more than half had moved
> to the new factory. These workers thought that if people
> at the old factory were compensated, they (those who had
> gone to the new factory) would also be compensated. Plus
> they would have work and overtime. Everyone thought of
> it like that. The management all told us it was the same
> as the fight for the funds last year. They said that the new
> factory hadn't even undergone a strike and still got their
> funds compensated. Many people thought this time would
> be the same.[22]

The methods that the bosses and government used to divide the workers were effective, but it seems they never considered that even without those workers who "didn't really contribute," the remaining 370 workers would continue to hold out for more than forty days.

Petitioning the Provincial Capital

In contrast to the December strike, the workers were in a passive position from the beginning of the June strike. There were several reasons for this.

First, the workers had not prepared at all, and the employers had moved the important machinery, materials, and products in advance. They also took care of the combative male workers in order to weaken the workers.

Second, the employers had a plan in place when they provoked the strike. They had the police come forward and "kidnap" a female worker who became their "hostage."

Third, the management tricked more than four hundred workers into going to the new factory to further weaken the workers.

Fourth, the workers were forced into the fight, and the responses they organized during the first several days were completely ineffective. They did not succeed in "rescuing the hostage," and they had no bargaining chips because occupying the factory did not put enough economic pressure on the employers. Although they progressed to petitioning government offices in only a few short days, they then ran into a brick wall. The idea of using the government to put pressure on the management produced no results.

Beginning on the 15th, the strike settled into a deadlock that was completely unfavorable to the workers. While the workers continued to defend the factory and stopped the management from moving the remaining equipment, they also continued to petition the subdistrict office and district government. In addition, the workers released a public announcement on June 21 in the hopes of drawing greater attention. On June 23, they put up a banner in the factory and did a sit-in protest.

Although actions were necessary in order to maintain morale, under these circumstances, occupying the factory and visiting the local-level government was only sufficient to stop the collective from immediately dissolving. Furthermore, appeals to the "society" and playing the underdog in the factory had no effect. The employers and government, meanwhile, were taking steps to close in on the workers. The employers marked them as absentees to put psychological pressure on the workers, and the government began to clearly declare the workers' futile actions to be violating the law. On the 25th, the police sent officers to seize two workers' delegates from their homes.

To break them out, there had to be another collective action. A spirited struggle would have been a powerful counterattack, but the two weeks of striking had left the middle-aged women physically exhausted. The delays, deceptions, insults, and intimidations they experienced over the course of the strike left some workers grief-stricken. At this point, a new group of activist workers stepped forward. After confidential discussions with the original workers' delegates, they decided to split their forces. The new group would take more than a hundred workers to secretly petition provincial government offices. The original workers' delegates would stay with the other workers and "watch over things."

On the morning of the 29th, more than a hundred workers hurried to the specified meeting place and took two rented buses to petition the provincial capital. Preventing citizens from petitioning higher levels of government is a security maintenance task for local governments. After two strikes, while under surveillance, over one hundred workers succeeded in reaching the gates of the Provincial Petitions Office. Not just the workers themselves, but many others who were following this strike were extremely excited. No matter the result, this was superbly executed; not a single other Pearl River Delta strike in recent years has been able to make its way to the provincial government offices. Almost all strikes that reach the municipal government level hit a wall and exhaust the workers' resources.

The workers assumed there would be results the same day they petitioned, but their hopes were in vain. They encountered the same response as when they petitioned the municipal government and all of the government departments they spoke to perfunctorily delayed the issue.

Although the attitude of the provincial government was unclear, the petition had already put great pressure on the employers and local government. The employers agreed to negotiate with the workers almost immediately. They scheduled a preparatory meeting on June 30 and a formal negotiation on July 1. The local police's "seizure team" (*zhuabudui*) had arrived at the provincial capital at almost the same time as the workers. However, perhaps because the workers had consciously avoided gathering together or because the seizure team still didn't have permission from the provincial government, they simply sent plainclothes officers to accompany the workers and did not take them from the streets.

The workers were thrilled when the employers agreed to negotiate. The workers who had originally planned to return the same day decided they would stay in the provincial capital until the negotiations bore results.

On July 2, the boss who had never once shown his face finally came to the negotiating table. Still, his attitude was inflexible. He insisted, "There is no provision in the law that I have to compensate you if I relocate the factory." During the second round of negotiations that afternoon, the boss unilaterally announced he was ending the discussions and demanded that the workers consult with the company on an individual basis. He never again showed his face.

Because the petitioners had originally planned to return to the factory within one day, they did not bring enough money with them. Lodging and accommodations quickly became a problem. After a discussion, everyone agreed to hold a public fundraiser. They put up a sign on the street, opened a bank account at a local bank, and asked online supporters for assistance. Even with the donations, most of the workers had to rough it and slept in the streets from June 29 to July 5. In truth, the workers could have had friends and families take care of their daily expenses. That is to say, the workers' families were not without resources, but they thought a fundraiser would increase their influence and lend them more attention and support from the society at large. Police confiscated the bank card on July 6, before the donations were fully spent. After the failure of the strike, the worker who had opened the account was too scared to go to the bank and report the card lost, so the remaining sum still has not been withdrawn.

On the morning of Monday, July 6, the workers went once again to the provincial Bureau of Letters and Calls. After submitting their materials, they waited until the afternoon, but there was no activity. Having not yet been arrested, the workers let their guard down and entered the bureau's great hall together to wait. There they were easily seized (*bao le jiaozi*) by cops from City S. It was only later that they learned that the employee who had taken the workers' materials that morning was in fact from City S. The provincial authorities had lent him a uniform, and he pretended to be a provincial employee in order to trick the workers into giving him their documents.

At around five o'clock on July 6, all of the workers were loaded onto a police bus. Upon arriving at City S, they were taken to the police department, where records were made. They were not released until two o'clock the next morning.

The climax of the June strike had concluded.

The Failure of the June Strike

Industrial transformation and improvement is an established government policy. Following the outbreak of the factory relocation strikes, the government suppressed workers' demands in order to forward this policy and preserve the bosses' profits.

Although the provincial authorities expressed no standpoint, they assisted those from City S in deceiving the workers into submitting their materials. They also allowed people from the local government to seize people in the great hall of the Bureau of Letters and Calls. These actions clearly demonstrate the problem. Moreover, the struggle of these factory workers to maintain their rights had already aroused the support of some international labor groups and of some so-called labor scholars and others within the country. It was having an influence. Therefore, they could not let it succeed. Specifically, they could not let this group, which had brought their dispute all the way to the provincial government, succeed, lest it set an example for countless other workers fighting for their rights and cause more workers to "raise a ruckus." This case could not be opened; this wind could not be allowed to grow (*ci feng bu ke zhang*).

But the provincial government did not directly suppress the workers. When workers from a small factory stand up for their rights, they are supposed to disappear on the spot. Now they had come all the way to the provincial government, showing that the local government was inept. If the provincial authorities had stepped in, it would have undoubtedly fueled the flames and may have increased the impact of this incident. It's also possible that it would have provoked the already excited workers. So, they simply used underhanded methods to deceive the workers into submitting their petitioning materials and then pretended they were unaware. They claimed to have no knowledge and waited for the local government to take care of the mess.

To the boss, the attitude of the provincial authorities was clear. He knew that compromise was unacceptable. As for the local government, with the support of the provincial authorities, they were free to blithely "swindle" the workers.

Beginning on July 7, the employers and local government personnel began to harass the workers. The employers installed numerous cameras inside and outside the factory to monitor the workers who were keeping watch. The government sent people to the factory daily to announce the government's policies and used a high-volume loudspeaker to broadcast twenty-four hours per day. While threatening the workers, they discredited the labor NGO and rights-defense lawyers.

A succession of local government departments came to the factory to post notices saying that, because the strike was illegal, each of the workers' demands would be rejected. At this point, open signals were being sent out that the strike was being oppressed.

On July 14, police forces that claimed to be assisting an

investigation detained four workers' delegates.

On July 15, riot police went to the factory and assisted the employers in forcibly relocating the factory. Seven workers were taken to the police station, among whom two were further escorted to a detainment center. Only four workers were released that evening.

On July 16, there were police everywhere, both within and around the factory: "More than there were workers." Pedestrians walking by were seized for taking photos. The boss of a nearby pharmacy was detained by police merely for complaining that "if the factory's boss doesn't take care of this, no wonder the workers refuse to comply. The road blockage is affecting my business." Later, the health department also investigated the pharmacy.

The atmosphere of terror created on July 15 and 16 exceeded that of December 18 during the previous year. The workers on-site were not allowed to gather together and speak, and even looking at a police officer's eyes was considered provocation. This time, it was not only the workers' delegates and activists; each employee felt that he or she might be seized.

The management exploited their advantage to put forth a so-called "care fund" (guan'aijin) proposal: those who had worked less than ten years would receive five hundred yuan per year worked, those who had worked less than fifteen years would receive six hundred, and those who had worked more than fifteen years would receive eight hundred. This proposal was much lower than the legally stipulated standard for economic compensation.

In order to have the workers accept this plan and willingly sign resignations, the management first called all the workers and then went directly to their apartments. They sent plainclothes officers to intimidate the "stubborn elements," saying, "Either sign or you're going to the station."

The police forces and owner also used releases as bait. Like kidnappers, they forced those who had been detained to urge others to sign. Some workers did not believe that everyone would be released if the signatures were submitted, but other workers scolded them for not caring about those who had been detained and said they were heartless. Fierce arguments broke out between these two groups. In the end, the truth was its own evidence; they had no intention of releasing people. Worker F, who had been seized on the first day, was held for a total of four months and only released when she had signed a confession and been sentenced.

While the workers were beset by internal strife, a constant string of people was signing the "surrender." The management announced on the 21st that by July 20th, 278 workers had completed the official resignation process. On July 23, the last workers signed their names.

The June strike came to an end. It was hard for many of the women to accept this result. One worker reported that, after she went home, she was unable to eat or sleep for the next two weeks because she couldn't stop thinking about what had happened during the strike. She said she couldn't make any sense of it. She had worked honestly her entire life and never done anything bad, so why did it now seem she must have acted like a thief to have reached such a fate?

There were also several dozen workers who could not accept the results and collectively began a lawsuit. Two trials and a year and a half later, they still lost everything. As an additional note, none of the workers' delegates and almost none of the activists communicated with their former colleagues after the strike failed. They did not keep in touch with the organization that helped them or participate in any other collective demands.

Final Words

Besides the state, there is currently no other external force that can decisively influence the collective struggle of the working class. This is a basic fact of Chinese labor relations.

With or without outside assistance, the workers of this

strike had no trouble collecting the necessary information from all kinds of channels, summarizing general demands, spreading publicity, encouraging, and ultimately instigating collective action. In truth, almost all of the strikes in recent years have arisen in this way.

Organizations are able to make contact with and influence only a small number of militant workers. Once collective action breaks out, it is impossible for workers' delegates or activists to control the actions of most workers. Speaking frankly, this strike would still be classified as a spontaneous action, for the workers lacked even the most basic level of organization. From this perspective, there is no essential difference between this strike and the one that took place in 2013.

Notes

1. For evidence of this, see "China Is Not to Blame for the Decline of the US Working Class," by Eli Friedman (Truth-out.org, February 10, 2017, http://www.truth-out.org/opinion/item/39366-china-is-not-to-blame-for-the-decline-of-the-us-working-class) or *A Brief History of Neoliberalism,* by David Harvey.

2. For an introduction to the group, see the preface to "The Future Is Hidden within These Realities: Selected Translations from Factory Stories," in *Chuang #1: Dead Generations* (2016), http://chuangcn.org /journal/one/the-future-is-hidden-within-these-realities/ (accessed May 23, 2017). For translations of other selections from Factory Stories, see *Gongchao,* http://www.gongchao.org/en/factory-stories/ (accessed May 23, 2017).

3. *China Labour Bulletin* maintains a strike map (http://maps.clb.org.hk /strikes/en) based on a sampling of online reports of strikes. It is by no means comprehensive, but provides some indication of how widespread worker unrest is. For a discussion of other relevant data, see "Interview on Recent Trends: Labor Struggles, Organizing, and Repression in China," on Gongchao.org, http://www.gongchao.org/2016/06/01 /interview-struggles-organizing-repression (accessed July 8, 2017).

4. See "The Criminalization of Strikes since 2012" (http://chuangcn. org/2015/10/the-criminalization-of-strikes/), "Labour activist Wu Guijun detained for one year" (http://bit.ly/2tjfZfr), "Theses on the December 3 crackdown" (http://chuangcn.org/2015/12/theses-on-dec-3/), and "Chinese Police Detain Activist Who Documents Labor Protests" (https://www.nytimes.com/2016/06/28/world/asia/china-lu-yuyu-detain.html).

5. Editor's note: Throughout this book, "someone from my hometown" is used to translate *laoxiang.* This term actually means someone from the same place, which could be anything from a village to a country, depending on context. "Hometown" is used because other translations

would sound awkward, but in most cases it probably means people from the same province.

6. Editor's note: In China, when a workplace relocates to another city, the company is legally required to offer employees compensation should they choose not to transfer to the new workplace. That is why this demand is translated as "relocation compensation" rather than "severance pay," although the concept is similar and is likewise calculated as one month's wage for each year of employment at the workplace. In addition, the workers also used this strike to demand previously unpaid contributions to their Social Insurance accounts and other guaranteed benefits, such as high-temperature subsidies.

7. Editor's note: Throughout this book "casual workers" refers to a category of workers without contracts, usually hired for a temporary project or during a sudden personnel shortage, but hired directly by the factory; in contrast, agency workers have contracts with an agency.

8. Translator's note: A private armed force hired by police departments in Shenzhen's industrial districts, mainly to deal with labor disputes and riots.

9. Translator's note: Some cities in China limit the operating hours of certain industries to decrease the load on the power grid.

10. "Common workers" (*pugong*) are basic-level, semi-skilled, shop-floor workers who are paid basic wages, as opposed to foremen (*zuzhang*) and skilled workers or master craftsmen (*shifu*).

11. Editor's note: China's Social Insurance system includes five programs (the Pension System, Medical Insurance, Unemployment Insurance, Work-Related Injury Insurance, and Maternity Insurance) that are funded by contributions from both employer and employee. For details, see "China's Social Insurance System," http://www.clb.org.hk/content /china%E2%80%99s-social-security-system (accessed March 6, 2017).

12. This calculation of a daily salary uses a monthly payable term of 21.75 days rather than the actual working days of that calendar month. Cited at: https://www.lexology.com/library/detail.aspx?g=c66296b0-9c97 -474e-9417-0c4c0896626c.

13. This is a widely implemented government media help line. See for example: http://en.jsq.sh.gov.cn/news_detail.asp?id=1216.

14. Editor's note: The Housing Fund is technically separate from China's five Social Insurance programs and is administered by a different state ministry, but it functions similarly, with contributions paid jointly by workers and their employers. "Contributors to the housing fund can apply for preferential rate mortgages, cover housing repair and maintenance

costs, and get rent subsidies. If unused, the fund can be redeemed upon retirement, and as such it actually functions more as a secondary pension" ("China's Social Insurance System," op. cit.). Together, the six programs are referred to as the "five insurances and one fund" (*wu xian yi jin*).

15. Editor's note: The "Special Police" (*tejing*) are a SWAT unit of China's Armed Police Force, similar to, but separate from, the riot police.

16. Translator's note: In China, an intravenous drip of saline and antibiotics is a common treatment for colds.

17. Translator's note: one *mu* equals about one-sixth of an acre.

18. Translator's note: One *jin* equals half a kilogram.

19. Interview with one of the workers.

20. Interview with one of the workers.

21. Interview with one of the workers.

22. Interview with one of the workers.

Index

"Passim" (literally "scattered") indicates intermittent discussion of a topic over a cluster of pages.

About Haymarket Books

Haymarket Books is a radical, independent, nonprofit book publisher based in Chicago.

Our mission is to publish books that contribute to struggles for social and economic justice. We strive to make our books a vibrant and organic part of social movements and the education and development of a critical, engaged, international left.

We take inspiration and courage from our namesakes, the Haymarket martyrs, who gave their lives fighting for a better world. Their 1886 struggle for the eight-hour day—which gave us May Day, the international workers' holiday—reminds workers around the world that ordinary people can organize and struggle for their own liberation. These struggles continue today across the globe—struggles against oppression, exploitation, poverty, and war.

Since our founding in 2001, Haymarket Books has published more than five hundred titles. Radically independent, we seek to drive a wedge into the risk-averse world of corporate book publishing. Our authors include Noam Chomsky, Arundhati Roy, Rebecca Solnit, Angela Y. Davis, Howard Zinn, Amy Goodman, Wallace Shawn, Mike Davis, Winona LaDuke, Ilan Pappé, Richard Wolff, Dave Zirin, Keeanga-Yamahtta Taylor, Nick Turse, Dahr Jamail, David Barsamian, Elizabeth Laird, Amira Hass, Mark Steel, Avi Lewis, Naomi Klein, and Neil Davidson. We are also the trade publishers of the acclaimed Historical Materialism Book Series and of Dispatch Books.

Also Available from Haymarket Books

Autoworkers Under the Gun: A Shop-Floor View of the End of the American Dream
Gregg Shotwell, Afterword by Lee Sustar,
Foreword by Jerry Tucker

Bananeras: Women Transforming the Banana Unions of Latin America
Dana Frank

Building Global Labor Solidarity in a Time of Accelerating Globalization
Edited by Kim Scipes

China on Strike: Narratives of Workers' Resistance
Edited by Hao Ren, English-language edition edited by Eli Friedman and Zhongjin Li

Disposable Domestics: Immigrant Women Workers in the Global Economy
Grace Chang, Foreword by Alicia Garza,
Afterword by Ai-jen Poo

Live Working or Die Fighting: How the Working Class Went Global
Paul Mason

Rank and File: Personal Histories by Working-Class Organizers
Alice and Staughton Lynd

Urban Revolt: State Power and the Rise of People's Movements in the Global South
Edited by Immanuel Ness, Trevor Ngwane, and Luke Sinwell

About the Author

Fan Shigang was born into a family of workers for state-owned enterprises in a northern Chinese city. He has worked as a basic-level employee in several machining factories. He is a contributor to the underground labor periodical *Factory Stories*, conducting interviews with factory workers in southern China, documenting their lives, work, and struggles.